The Contented Achiever
How to Get What You Want
and Love What You Get

What people are saying about *The Contented Achiever* . . .

"We all prize success, yet often fail to recognize or understand it. *The Contented Achiever* helps with both."
> -- R. Brad Martin, Chairman and CEO
> Saks Incorporated, New York, New York

"This is a wonderful book that gives a step-by-step system to achieve better balance, more results and greater satisfaction in life and work than you ever thought possible."
> -- Brian Tracy
> Professional Speaker, Author, Solano Beach, California

"This book will touch people's lives in both the work and personal arena. Who doesn't need a mirror for reflection about the most important choices? Life is one decision after another, and *The Contented Achiever* helps make them clearer and easier."
> -- Dianna Booher, Author of *Communicate with Confidence*
> and *Well Connected*, Colleyville, Texas

"It is difficult for many people today to capture a life of both high achievement and peace of mind. *The Contented Achiever* is the road map. Great book!"
> -- Jack Soden, President & CEO
> Elvis Presley Enterprises, Memphis, Tennessee

"This book is especially appropriate in today's environment where we have not placed adequate emphasis on character, faith and a proper belief system. I wish you had written – and I had read it – years ago."
> -- Robert L. Bailey, Chairman of the Board
> State Auto Insurance Companies, Columbus, Ohio

"It's been said that most people aim at nothing in life and hit it with amazing accuracy. Well, *The Contented Achiever* breaks that mold! It's a step-by-step success manual for not only getting what you want but, more importantly, WANTING what you get."
> -- Dr. Tony Alessandra
> Professional Speaker, Author, La Jolla, California

"Content can be pronounced two ways: conTENT and CONtent. The first represents being at peace with yourself. The second is evidence of substance within. This book will fill you with the CONtent and substance to lead you toward being conTENT in your life. Read it and achieve."
   -- Jim Cathcart
      Author, *The Acorn Principle*, La Jolla, California

"It's amazing what happens and how much easier life becomes when you focus on things that work. *The Contented Achiever* is a treasure for anyone seeking harmony and happiness."
   -- Dr. Jim Tunney, former NFL Referee
      Coauthor of *Chicken Soup for the Sports Fan Soul*,
      and NSA Speaker Hall of Fame, Carmel-by-the-Sea, California

"This book weaves a wonderful combination of wisdom, knowledge, introspection and humor. It will have a profound and renewing effect on anyone who reads it."
   -- Ian D. Robb, Senior Vice President
      Marsh, New York, New York

"A book that includes the insight of Don Hutson and his colleagues can only be a winner. Don is the consummate sales professional and a great teacher!"
   -- Elliott Server, Senior Vice President
      Morgan Stanley Dean Witter, New York, New York

"*The Contented Achiever* is filled with practical advice about regaining control of your life. A quick, enjoyable read, but content rich."
   -- Michael S. Starnes, Chairman & CEO
      M.S. Carriers, Memphis, Tennessee

"Your book beautifully illustrates 'achievement' and 'contentment', inspiring me to share it with others, over and over again. Thank you for writing it!"
   -- Dennis A. Mele, President
      Cleaners Hanger Corp., Palm Harbor, Florida

"This is a book of simple concepts with profound meaning. A great read for anyone seeking a life of purpose."
    -- Jerry Britton, President
        MiddleMarket Group, Textron Financial Corp., Atlanta, Georgia

"This informative, soon-to-be best seller can help everyone discover the often elusive answers to the question, 'How can I take control of my life?' Hutson, Crouch and Lucas combine their vast knowledge of business and sales with unparalleled skills as inspirational and motivational writers to create a masterpiece of simplicity and truth that can apply to anyone."
    -- David J. Bronczek, CEO
        FedEx Express, Memphis, Tennessee

"*The Contented Achiever* addresses an important area of people's lives that other books have overlooked – defining success on your own terms. This is a must read for those looking for greater fulfillment in their lives."
    -- Steve Booker, Vice President
        The Clorox Company, Oakland, California

"I predict *The Contented Achiever* will be a dynamic success. The authors make the reader examine his or her belief system in a simplistic way through personal examples that one can relate to. A must read for anyone wanting real success in life."
    -- J. Michael Drake, President and CEO
        Econocom-USA, Memphis, Tennessee

"The authors prove the adage, 'You are what you believe,' then lay out steps to discover how our belief system can provide a sound foundation for a successful and satisfying life."
    -- Ken Evans, Executive Vice President, Consumer Group
        RPM Inc., Charleston, South Carolina

"No one could read *The Contented Achiever* and not come away with something of value. The book deals with matters of importance to each of us and provides a framework for prioritization."
    -- Joe Orgill
        Orgill, Inc., Memphis Tennessee

The Contented Achiever

How to Get What You Want
and Love What You Get

Don Hutson
▼
Chris Crouch
▼
George Lucas

To contact the authors with comments or to inquire about
speaking, seminars, or consulting, write to them at:

DLHutson@aol.com
CCSeagull888@aol.com
GeorgeUSL@aol.com

Copyright© 2001 by Don Hutson, Chris Crouch and George Lucas

Published by Black Pants Publishing, LLC
3410 S. Tournament Drive
Memphis, TN 38125

Editorial: Susan Drake
Typography: Colleen Wells
Cover Design: Lightbourne

Man's Search for Meaning by Viktor E. Frankl© 1959, 1962, 1984, 1992 by
Viktor E. Frankl. Reprinted by permission of Beacon Press, Boston.

Publisher's Cataloging-in-Publication
(Provided by Quality Books, Inc.)

Hutson, Don, 1945-
      The contented achiever : how to get what you want and love what you get
/ Don Hutson, Chris Crouch, George Lucas -- 1st ed.
      p. cm.
      LCCN: 00-109185
      ISBN: 0-9703736-3-5

1. Success 2. Satisfaction 3. Self-actualization (Psychology) 1.Crouch, Chris
II. Lucas, George H. III. Title

BF637.S8H88 2001   158.1
                                          QB100-850

This book is printed on acid-free paper.

Table of Contents

Acknowledgements

When the three of us decided to write a book together, it was like dropping ping-pong balls onto a hardwood floor. We bounced around all over the place. We were so excited! We were having so much fun! We bounced ideas off the walls, off each other and off the pages of our notebooks. We had some high-energy meetings and launched this book project with a tremendous amount of enthusiasm. Fortunately for us, that enthusiasm never waned. This project was a true source of joy for the three of us. The bad news . . . it is hard to cast a net over "bouncing creativity" and capture enough coherent words and phrases to turn it into a publishable book. The good news . . . we knew two extraordinary people named Susan Drake and Robin Thomas.

We will be forever grateful to Susan for taking thoughts, ideas and rough drafts from the three of us and helping harmonize them into one meaningful voice. She did a superb job of editing our work and making great suggestions. Because of her special gifts and talents, we were able to achieve our goal of writing a book much sooner than we anticipated and we remained contented throughout the process. Thank you Susan for capturing the bouncing words and phrases.

We suspect that the fantasy of many writers is to *only* have to write. Wouldn't it be nice if you could just type the words into a word processing program and somehow a book would magically appear? Unfortunately, the publishing world doesn't work that way. Getting the words into a word processor is the tip of the publishing iceberg. There are hundreds of minor and not so minor details that must be taken care of in order to give birth to a healthy baby book. And then the "word-child" must be constantly nurtured if it is to ever grow and journey out into the world of readers.

Once again, we were fortunate to find a person who made all of this essentially a two-step process. Our two steps included handing off all the publishing details to Robin Thomas and watching it happen! Robin's dedication and efforts to move this project forward have been extraordinary. She has worked endless hours taking care of all the important issues that must be handled to turn words into a book. Thank goodness for people like Robin who are as passionate about the publishing process as we are about the writing process. Thank you Robin for your knowledge, professionalism and dedication to our project.

And we thank you, the readers of the world, for choosing to share some time with us as you read *The Contented Achiever.* We are honored to be able to share our thoughts with you and hope this work contributes to both your contentment and achievement.

The Contented Achiever

How to Get What You Want
and Love What You Get

Introduction

Do you want to see things clearly, do things simply and live more peacefully? Certainly. We all do. But clarity, simplicity and peacefulness are words that seem out of place in the lives of 21st century planet riders. Confusion, complexity and chaos are more like it. In fact, our closest companions are often stress and anxiety. Yet in the middle of this complexity, we still occasionally encounter someone who is centered, calm, grounded, peaceful and highly successful. These people seem to attract success rather than chase after it. They never force things. They are always focused, energetic and give their full attention to the present moment. They are clearly in control of life, and are living a life of purpose and meaning. They are "Contented Achievers."

What are these people doing differently? What is their secret? How do they so effortlessly win the game of life? Are they aware of a unique set of rules or principles that apply to playing the game? Do they have a better understanding of these principles than others do? Do they know how to apply these principles more effectively in their daily lives? Not surprisingly, the answer to the last three questions is yes, yes, and yes. That is what this eight-chapter life guide is about. This book will help you reduce chaos, clarify success, focus your energy and gain peace of mind. It will help you become a "Contented Achiever."

Lights and Enlightenment

If a child saw you turning on the lights in a room and asked you how it works, you would probably explain that you simply flip the switch and the lights come on. This would be an appropriate response to a casual question from a child. An apprentice electrician, however, would need to know that there is much more to the story: electricity, wiring, circuit breakers and many other aspects of making lights go on. On a deeper level, someone else might need to understand the generation of power and how to transmit that power to outlying places.

Life operates in the same way. If you want to create a specific outcome in your life, you must have a deep understanding of how the laws that affect your life experience really work.

The goal of this book is to help you create the life that you want. You must not only have a superficial understanding of the unwritten principles that govern your life; you must, as Paul Harvey says, also know "the rest of the story."

Simple Is Better

The good news is, the more you break things down into their basic components, the simpler things get. Therefore, another goal of this book is to provide you with some very simple and effective guidelines to improve your life experience. Albert Einstein, *Time* magazine's "Man of the Century," said:

> *"Any intelligent fool can make things bigger, more complex, and more violent. It takes a touch of genius, and a lot of courage, to move in the opposite direction."*

As you read this book, keep in mind three key concepts that will help you "move in the opposite direction:"

- Awareness

- Understanding

- Application

Awareness is critically important; however, it is certainly not enough to create the life you desire. You must also have a profound understanding of the principles that influence your life. And, if you are serious about creating the life that you desire, you must become a master at applying your knowledge to daily events. By doing all three, you can get from where you are to where you want to be.

Many books are written primarily to raise your awareness of a particular issue. Other books are primarily written to deepen

The Contented Achiever

your understanding of an issue. This book addresses both of these issues and will help you take the all-important next step—applying what you have learned in your everyday life. Three authors collaborated on this work, and each has included personal stories and experiences. For ease of reading, however, we have written it from a single point of view. Through our combined outlook we hope you will learn to:

- Define success and stay on a path that will give you the greatest personal satisfaction.

- Create the specific results you desire in any area of your life.

- Direct your thoughts, words and actions to create favorable circumstances.

- Align your personal belief system with natural laws that govern your life.

- Eliminate mental and physical clutter from your life.

- Create a personal environment that's conducive to success.

- Discover ways to respond productively and appropriately to the people in your life.

- Put the pieces of the "puzzle called your life" together in a way that will provide you with freedom, growth and joy.

The Contented Achiever

Our mission in this book is to provide you with the clarity you need to become centered, calm, grounded, peaceful, and highly successful. Take the self-assessment in the back of this book and measure your contentment quotient. Then, using this book as a guide, begin to eliminate chaos and confusion, and become one of those rare people in life who have successfully made the journey from chaos to clarity. In short, you can become one of a small group of Contented Achievers, people who get what they want and love what they get.

> **"IF YOU FOLLOW YOUR BLISS, DOORS
> WILL OPEN FOR YOU THAT WOULDN'T
> HAVE OPENED FOR ANYONE ELSE."**
> JOSEPH CAMPBELL

The Contented Achiever

Chapter One
Defining Success:
The Journey Toward Intangibles

"Mistaken Certainty"

Have you ever had a bad case of mistaken certainty? Put yourself in this situation: You're playing poker, and you've just picked up the last hand of the evening. One by one you fan out your cards. King of hearts. King of diamonds. King of spades. Six of spades. You take a deep breath as you slowly reveal the last card. The fourth king! It's there! Imagine how you feel when you see that card. It's difficult to contain the euphoric feeling of certainty. You are going to win and you are going to win big. You maintain your best poker face and carefully bump up the stakes. The guy to your left foolishly raises your bet. You can't believe your luck -- you raise his raise. Finally the last bet is down and it's time to show your cards. You lay down your four kings and tell your opponents to "read 'em and weep!" And then, as you reach for your winnings, the unthinkable happens: The guy to your left tables four aces. FOUR ACES! Wait, there was no way you could lose! But you did. As the other person drags his winnings toward him, you suddenly understand what the concept of mistaken certainty is all about.

Are You Certain?

Mistaken certainty is as common as the common cold. You've probably experienced it from time to time, or, at the very least, you know someone who has. Your spouse insists that you should turn left on Oak Street to get to the restaurant. Your grandfather swears that your grandmother was wearing a red dress when he met her instead of blue. Your teenager insists that Van Halen invented rock 'n' roll. They all believe that without any doubt they are right. No need for further discussion or debate. There is absolutely no possibility that they could be wrong. There's only one problem: The passage of time and the unfolding of events prove that -- THEY ARE DEAD WRONG!

U–Turns in Life

It's usually no big deal to be wrong about a poker hand or a left turn, because they're relatively unimportant in the overall scheme of things. But you can also suffer mistaken cer-

The Contented Achiever

tainty about bigger, more painful things like well . . . like the meaning of success. In fact, many people work very hard to climb the ladder of success, and suddenly find that their ladder is leaning against the wrong wall.

It is human nature -- at least in our society -- to think that the person with the most material possessions or highest community status is the most successful. We are taught from birth to strive, and all of our striving is

IMPLICIT WITH ACHIEVING SUCCESS IS THE EXPECTATION OF FEELING FULFILLED OR HAPPY.

supposed to have an easily recognizable result: good grades, popularity, a winning football season, a hot car and a big house. We are taught to be "destination seekers," defining success in terms of events that will occur or tangibles that will be acquired some time in the future. "Destination seekers" think that when one or more of their strivings is accomplished, they will have arrived at the destination they call success. And implicit with achieving success is the expectation of feeling fulfilled or happy.

I have friends who are considered highly successful by society, but at the same time are experiencing distress, sorrow, and strong internal feelings of restlessness. Many of them thought when they achieved a certain status in the community or attained certain possessions on their wish list they'd be assured of fulfillment. But then they got exactly what they wanted in life and suddenly found themselves asking, as Peggy Lee once sang . . . "Is that all there is?"

Getting There and Discovering Emptiness

It's possible (and probable) that when you get exactly what you wish for, you'll be in for the surprise of your life. When you finally "arrive" at what you consider to be your goal or destination, you will learn the meaning of mistaken certainty.

Why does this happen? One possible answer is that you focused on something that doesn't truly bring you joy and fulfillment. You thought you would be happy when you achieved a certain goal; however, you were "mistakenly certain" about how you would feel when you arrived.

Achievements and acquisitions are common and excellent byproducts of true success. However, for most of us, they're just not enough to define true success. To be genuinely successful you must have happiness, joy and fulfillment in your life.

For Richer, For Poorer

Are wealth and fulfillment mutually exclusive? Certainly not. One of the basic desires in life is to have the freedom to make choices without regard to monetary consequences. There is

The Contented Achiever

no better way of doing this than by generating enough wealth to consistently exceed the monetary demands of your lifestyle. When you do this, you are free to make choices without considering money. And that freedom, although not required to live a truly successful life, "is a great way to go!"

Of course, the freedom train can quickly derail when you begin to define how much money is enough. People who make $20,000 a year think they would be happy if they made $40,000 a year. People who make $1 million want $5 million. In each case, once people arrive at their original target, it doesn't produce an enduring feeling of happiness. At that point people usually do one of two things:

1. Advance the target: If it isn't $40,000, then maybe it's $50,000. I'll just make more.

2. Add a new goal: Now that I have money, I just need a new title, job, hobby, spouse . . . or, fill in the unmet desire of your choice here.

After repeated attempts to fix the problem with different "stuff," a person may decide that the problem may not be to get "more" stuff, but perhaps "different" stuff.

Strangely enough, the person who makes $10,000 a year and lives on $8,000 a year can be richer than the person who makes $300,000 a year and spends $350,000.

Extreme Thinking

One of the easiest ways to clarify any idea is to look at it in terms of extremes or opposites. Look at the following diagram. The line is a simple continuum that shows failure at one end and success at the other.

FAILURE ————————————— SUCCESS

Few people start at absolute "failure;" however, we will start there to help emphasize the extreme positions. (And we won't assume that our society has correctly identified who is a failure and who is not. Was Thomas Edison a failure for the many times he discovered how not to make a light bulb?) Great writers and philosophers have said that the journey is more important than the destination; so, let's start by thinking of this diagram as a journey. If you plan to go on a journey, one of the first things you need to do is decide upon a direction. In the diagram, most people, no matter where they start on the line, prefer to go from left to right, toward success and away from failure.

FAILURE ————————————→ SUCCESS

As time passes, however, we all tend to travel back and forth between the extremes of success and failure. This is a normal progression for most people as we encounter obstacles and ego-related issues on our way to our destination.

The Contented Achiever

The Second Dimension

Now consider another dimension of success, and add to the chart two more dynamics that are also involved in the Journey of Life . . . fulfillment and frustration.

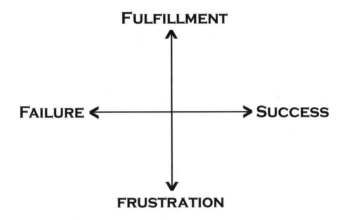

Again we've illustrated this continuum with extremes or opposites. And just as you move back and forth between failure and success, you probably also vacillate between feelings of fulfillment and frustration. Some days, life is great. You're enjoying work and have a real sense of accomplishment and contribution, your family is happy, and your golf game couldn't be better. The next day, your computer crashes, you miss a big deadline, you have an argument with your teenager, and you can't hit anything straight. Fulfillment to frustration -- overnight. Fortunately, life goes on, and the next day a few things fall back into place and you're once again moving in the direction of fulfillment.

The Contented Achiever

Failure to success, frustration to fulfillment: Life consists of all four extremes, as well as many degrees in between. Combine them, and you'll see that life's journey has four quadrants, each representing a combination of material failure and success, as well as frustration and fulfillment.

Let's consider the characteristics of each and see which one you feel most comfortable with.

Quadrant 1: Soap Opera People

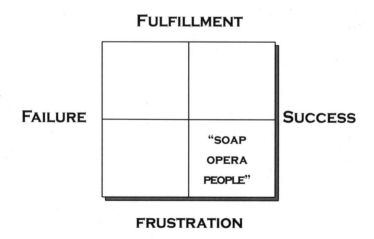

Have you ever watched a soap opera? Never have so many had so much and been so miserable. These martini-sipping, designer-clad, gadabout men and women are caricatures of wealthy, dissatisfied, "successful" people. We laugh at the

The Contented Achiever

exaggeration and contradiction, but these people don't exist just in television. Look around. How many people do you see in your circle who are obsessively pursuing a goal: a higher rank in government, a bigger house, a more prestigious office, smarter children, more expensive toys.

We'll call these the "Soap Opera People." These people are considered highly successful in the traditional sense, but are often quite frustrated with their lives. Many have busily pursued material items only to find that their compulsive pursuit results more in stress and frustration than fulfillment and joy.

Quadrant 2: Tar Pit People

Our next choice to consider is the bottom left quadrant . . . frustration and failure. These are the "Tar Pit People." They are stuck, bogged down and usually immobilized.

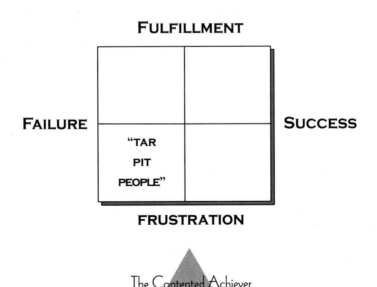

FULFILLMENT

FAILURE   **SUCCESS**

"TAR PIT PEOPLE"

FRUSTRATION

Tar Pit People have neither material success nor emotional fulfillment. They can't get ahead, they don't know what to do about it, and invariably, if they take any steps, the steps seldom lead to either goal. Not a very pleasant place to be.

Quadrant 3: Oxymoron People

The top left quadrant is a most interesting life situation -- fulfilled and a material failure. These are people who might be designated a failure by society, but who have actually discovered some of the key aspects to fulfillment in life. We'll call these the "Oxymoron People."

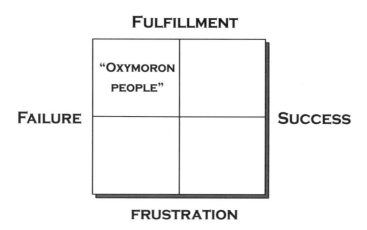

Oxymoron People may be artists, writers, engineers, parents of a dozen foster children, third-world missionaries. They may be people who have achieved little materially, but who are happy pursuing their passion in life. By the world's stan-

The Contented Achiever

dards, they may be unsuccessful, but by their own standards they are living the life they choose, and feeling happy about their accomplishments.

Quadrant 4: Contented Achievers

That leaves us with the top right quadrant: people who have managed to become both fulfilled and materially successful. They are doing what they enjoy and being paid well for it. We will simply call them "Contented Achievers."

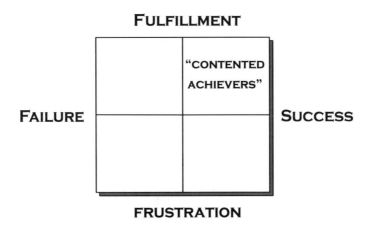

FULFILLMENT

"CONTENTED ACHIEVERS"

FAILURE   **SUCCESS**

FRUSTRATION

Take Your Pick

Want to hear some great news? You can choose the life quadrant where you want to be. So which will you pick?

The Contented Achiever

Would you choose to be with the Soap Opera People in the bottom right quadrant -- materially successful and frustrated? Surely you will say a resounding, "No!"

> CONTENTED ACHIEVERS HAVE IT ALL: THE ABILITY TO BE RICH AND ENJOY IT.

What about getting stuck with the Tar Pit People? If you did not quickly vote NO to this quadrant, give this book to someone else, or put it away for now and read it in a few years.

Would you like to be in the Oxymoron group? If this is your choice, you may have already arrived. Enjoy your success!

And finally, we consider taking up residence with the Contented Achievers. Hey, this is where we want to be! This quadrant offers the potential for both material benefit and a sense of self-fulfillment. Contented Achievers live in the moment and focus on the day-to-day activities that allow them to use their unique gifts and talents to generate the money necessary to support their lifestyle. They know that success is not in the future, it is now. They have it all: the ability to be rich and enjoy it.

Do You Need Double Vision?

To become a Contented Achiever, you must focus on balancing all of the elements that will help you create a successful life. But how will you find the time and energy to focus on both riches and happiness?

This is your first big clue: Focusing on material possessions and destinations will not assure that you will become successful and fulfilled.

A Kodak Moment

Let's use that clue to discover what will drive you into the contented achiever quadrant. When you look at photo negatives, everything that you thought was dark in the real world is light, and everything you thought was light is dark. Sometimes the photo lab will actually print the pictures backwards and left-handed people become right-handed. Everything is the opposite of what it appears to be.

The universe we live in often presents the same illusion as a photo negative, creating a backwards picture of reality. This illusion may cause us to draw erroneous conclusions about the way the world works. Here's an example of how things can be just the opposite of the way they appear: You may think that to forgive someone is a benevolent act that primarily benefits the other person. After becoming angry with some-one, you may think . . . I'm going to do that person a favor and forgive them, and then they'll feel better.

To figure out what reality is, think of the exact opposite, that you are really doing yourself a favor by letting go of any anger and resentment toward the other person. This opposite view can bring new meaning to the saying, "Resentment does more damage to the vessel in which it is stored than to the object upon which it is poured."

"RESENTMENT DOES MORE DAMAGE TO THE VESSEL IN WHICH IT IS STORED THAN TO THE OBJECT UPON WHICH IT IS POURED."

Anger and resentment not only create a significant amount of mental and physical stress, but deprive you of that precious commodity we call fulfillment. Truly forgiving someone allows you to let go of these feelings of resentment and return to a more healthy state of mind and body. The resentful person is always the primary beneficiary of the act of forgiveness.

This is one example of how the world often seems to get things backwards. Looking at things the way they really are, rather than the way they appear: Now that's truly a Kodak moment!

The Contented Achiever

Outlook Determines Outcomes

How can we turn the success equation around? If most people believe that we should pursue possessions alone and focus on destinations to be successful, let's look at an opposite, and possibly better alternative. What are some things we could focus on besides material wealth? (By the way, we're not looking for the "right answer." There are many "right answers.") Here are a few good possibilities to consider:

- Focus on having fun and joy in your life

- Focus on the personal freedom that will allow you to make good life choices

- Focus on personal growth and learning

- Focus on being creative and artistic

- Focus on being associated with high quality

- Focus on serving and enriching the lives of others

Perhaps you think these answers sound too simple. Don't underestimate the power of an idea because of its simplicity. These are often the best ideas. One of my favorite Einstein quotes is, "Make everything as simple as possible but no simpler." Pick one of the above ideas and ask yourself. . . "If I truly focus on this idea, what will happen in my life?"

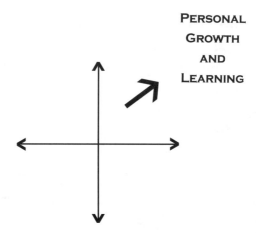

For example, consider what might happen if you focus on personal growth and learning. You pick the topic. It could be acting, music, teaching, business, flying, painting, or any other area of knowledge. Truly focus on the topic and develop a profound knowledge of it. I am talking about a "no holding back dedication" to the pursuit of knowledge in your chosen area. You will experience one of two possible outcomes:

1. If you develop a profound understanding of any body of knowledge, you can probably easily command material items such as money in exchange for your knowledge. They are a natural by-product, and will easily flow into your life.

2. The other possibility is that you will not care about the by-products. Like the actor who just wants to act, the painter who just wants to paint, the musician who just

wants to create music, you would be highly successful. It may not look like it to others who measure success in terms of tangibles and status; however, you would enjoy your pursuits in the moment.

So, strange as it may seem, while focusing on material possessions and destinations will not assure that you will become fulfilled, focusing on being fulfilled can assure that you are materially successful!

> **"WHEN YOU DON'T CONSIDER MONEY,**
> **YOU MAKE THE RIGHT CHOICE, AND THE**
> **RIGHT CHOICE ALWAYS LEADS TO MONEY."**
> JERRY SEINFELD

A Not-So-Starving Artist

What is it like to be a top right quadrant person, the "Contented Achiever," someone who has it all? I believe the book *Jonathan Livingston Seagull* provides one of the best examples of a person (or bird in this case) in this quadrant.

In the beginning of the book, thousands of seagulls are waiting on the beach for "breakfast flock," the time of day when the fishermen off shore threw chum into the water. When I first read this passage, I did not know much about chum. However, I knew that if the fishermen were throwing it away, it must not be one of the more desirable parts of the fish.

When I learn a new word, I often try to work it into a conversation over the next few days. I never really felt like doing this with the word chum. When I asked my fisherfriends about chum, they referred to it as garbage. That's why I found it fascinating that the seagulls were so excited about breakfast flock. As the fishermen tossed the chum overboard, the seagulls would scratch and claw and fight each other to get a piece of garbage. They lived for and were totally controlled by the fishermen and their chum. They were totally focused on the tangible called chum. The pursuit of chum expanded in their lives. It became their reason for living. As I read this, I developed a very clear picture of breakfast flock. I imagined thousands of seagulls on the beach scratching, clawing and fighting for pieces of garbage. It was not a pretty sight.

Far above them, Jonathan Livingston Seagull soared, practicing his life's passion . . . flying. He wasn't concerned with breakfast flock; he was clearly focused on increasing his skills and knowledge of flying. He was oblivious to the battle going on below because it had no real meaning to him. Because he had become highly skilled at flying, he could fly far inland and dine on delicate insects (the seagull version of gourmet cuisine) any time he desired. He learned to dive beneath the surface of the ocean and find an abundance of tasty fish. He no longer had to rely on the fisherman for his supply of food. Jonathan was free of the concerns of breakfast, lunch or din-

The Contented Achiever

ner flock. He was in charge of his own life, giving up the chaos of chasing fishermen with thousands of other gulls to passionately pursue his dream. Because Jonathan was focused on the intangible, never-ending journey to pursue flying excellence, the by-products came easily for him. Jonathan was no ordinary bird. Jonathan was clearly a top-right quadrant bird focused and in control of his destiny. He was successful and fulfilled. Jonathan was focused on achieving excellence, and received joy, satisfaction, success and fulfillment in his life. His life had meaning and purpose.

Flocking or Flying High?

Are you a member of the breakfast flock crowd, or are you a Jonathan Livingston Seagull? Are you totally controlled by the pursuit of tangibles and destinations? Or are you on a journey to passionately pursue your dreams? Are you focused on the by-products or the journey? What quadrant are you choosing? Do your choices lead to success and fulfillment, or do they take you toward failure and frustration?

Have you been a victim of mistaken certainty? Realizing that you may need to re-focus can be a wonderful opportunity for growth and positive change. Use your knowledge to fine-tune your focus, and to re-direct your efforts toward intangibles that bring you fulfillment. In this way you may find a peaceful balance that results in reaping some of the tangibles as well. Because pursuing wealth and tangibles as by-products of your passions in life is an excellent way to become "rich and famous" and actually enjoy it.

The Contented Achiever

POINTS TO PONDER

✖ Think about how you personally define success. Who are some of the most successful people you know? Why do you consider them successful?

✖ In which quadrant have you spent most of your life? What is your true focus in life and what will the by-products of that focus be?

✖ What is your passion in life (like flying for Jonathan) and how are you using it to create a successful life?

✖ What are your special gifts, skills and talents and how are you using them to create success in your life?

✖ What would it take for you to enjoy greater peace of mind at this time in your life?

✖ How do you approach success? Are you focused on tangibles and destinations or journeys and intangibles? Are you looking inside yourself or outside yourself for the key to success and fulfillment?

"REDUCE YOUR PLAN TO WRITING. THE MOMENT YOU COMPLETE THIS, YOU WILL HAVE DEFINITELY GIVEN CONCRETE FORM TO THE INTANGIBLE DESIRE."

NAPOLEON HILL

Chapter Two
Creating Desired Results:
Converting Thoughts and
Dreams into Action

Trust is an integral part of the human existence; however, do you know anyone who seems to have a hard time trusting other people? I do. I was thinking of that person the other day as I was sitting on an airplane during takeoff. The engines roared, everything started to vibrate and we began rolling down the runway. We were about to fly from Phoenix to Dallas. As we lifted off, it occurred to me how much we have to trust people, equipment, processes and many other things in order to calmly sit on an airplane (that someone else is controlling) as it rises to over 30,000 feet going several hundred miles an hour.

Luckily, I didn't get the fear-of-flying gene. Being a "window person," my main concern is the view. I'm still fascinated with majestic sights and watching things get smaller and smaller as we gain altitude. During takeoff, I never think about the condition of the aircraft, the skill of the pilot, or the risk I'm taking by putting my life in someone else's hands.

Now this is what is really strange. My friend -- the one who doesn't trust anyone or anything -- never hesitates to get on an airplane and put his life in the hands of a pilot. When I've flown with him, he seems totally unconcerned with the risk. He's normally focused on something like reading a newspaper or a magazine. What made the difference? Why would a person who has trouble trusting others, worries incessantly, and often makes a big fuss about seemingly minor things, be totally unconcerned about an event that could cost him his life if the pilot made a mistake, or the equipment failed?

How often have you boarded an airplane and put your trust in a total stranger in the cockpit? The first time you have any meaningful interaction with the pilot is when you arrive at the destination and he is standing in the cockpit door thanking you for choosing his airline. And you usually have no knowledge of the aircraft; you may not know a 727 from an L1011. It just happens to be the airplane the airline decides to use on the day you just happen to be going wherever it's going.

Ground Rules

Why are people willing to make such blind and trusting assumptions? I think you, I, and my non-trusting flying com-

The Contented Achiever

panion are unconcerned because we believe that the following conditions exist:

- The pilot (person in charge) is well trained and highly competent.

- The airline has a clear mission (safe travel to a specific destination).

- The equipment (resource) is suitable for the mission.

- The consequences of error or incompetence are the same for the pilot, the crew and the passengers (all our lives are at stake)!

There are clearly some parallels between flying an airplane, and running your life. The pilot is obviously the person in charge and the person ultimately responsible for success. Since you are the pilot of your life, you are in charge of arriving at your personal and professional destinations.

If Offices Were Airplanes

I thought about some of the largest organizations in the country with hundreds of offices in many states. I couldn't help but wonder . . . if all of these offices were airplanes, would I be so quick to hop on board and take a flight with the person in command? I believe most of these organizations have some of the best people in the business; however, I must admit that

I would hesitate to fly with many of them. I am perfectly willing to get on any airplane in the fleet and fly with a stranger in charge. I don't have the same comfort level with each office in the "fleet" of many well-established companies. And I'm not picking on any particular organization. I think this analogy applies to most businesses or organizations that we deal with daily.

So, can we convert the concepts behind a successful airline flight into actions that will help us achieve our goals? What can we all do in our everyday lives to help create the results we desire? How can we make our personal and professional "flights in life" successful? Can we create a "personal checklist" that works for us?

A Model for Success

Years ago I read a book by Robert Fritz called *The Path of Least Resistance*. Fritz's thoughts were simple yet very powerful. Powerful enough that I have not forgotten them in the 15 or 20 years since I read them. Fritz explained that if you want to create any desired result, you must have three things:

1. A clear vision of what you desire to accomplish.

2. An accurate assessment of your reality.

3. An action plan that will move you from your current reality to the vision.

Let's look at a simple model of this success pattern:

In chapter one we discussed the journey toward success, and how you can define success in a way that's right for you. Now let's look at this model as a guide to help you take the next step to create the specific results that you desire in your personal and professional life.

I call this the Creating Desired Results model. It helps you focus on the interim destinations that you'll need to make on your continuing journey toward success. Remember not to define any one of these single destinations as success. Like my flight from Phoenix to Dallas, life is full of interim destinations that move you toward your definition of success. Soon after I arrived in Dallas, I caught another flight to Atlanta, and ultimately went on to Birmingham. Dallas and Atlanta were just interim stops along the way. Similarly, in life you may experience many interim destinations . . . finishing high school, completing college, getting your first job, getting your first promotion, and on and on and on. None of these single destinations defines the success of your life. They are interim destinations along your journey of success.

Step One: Having Visions

Step one is to write a vision statement. One easy way to deal with the vision statement component of this model is to simply write down a statement of what it would look like if things were just the way you wanted them to be. If you want to create desired results in a business, describe the business as if everything is going perfectly. If you want to create a healthy relationship with someone, describe the perfect relationship. If you want to create a certain financial condition in your life, describe the financial situation that you desire. It doesn't matter what you desire. The first key to success is to paint a mental picture in your mind's eye of WHAT IT LOOKS LIKE WHEN THINGS ARE GOING EXACTLY THE WAY YOU WANT THEM TO GO. Then write your mental picture down and give yourself credit for completing step one.

Watch Out for Side Trips

Don't get stuck here trying to differentiate a vision from a mission from a goal or other planning buzzwords. Our business training might have us trying to develop a vision statement, a mission statement, a statement of objectives, a creed or some other type of document that explains what we're trying to accomplish. People get confused figuring out which statement should really drive their activities, or developing several statements for the same project. Let's just keep it simple. Stick with one statement and call it the vision state-

The Contented Achiever

ment for purposes of this model. That will allow us to minimize the confusion associated with multiple statements. If it's really important to you, change the name of this step to "mission statement," "statement of objectives," or "Fred" or "Wilma" for that matter. Just visualize your desired outcome and write it down to drive the model.

Personal Vision Statements

For decades organizations have struggled with their mission and vision statements. I have facilitated strategic planning retreats where ten to twenty managers have argued for over an hour over the choice between two different words for inclusion in the organization's statement. By contrast, I have worked with others where the golf tournament bets and pairings session lasted ten times longer than the vision statement consideration. You are probably saying to yourself that corporations need vision statements, but what is the deal with personal vision statements? Such statements can be an extraordinarily valuable tool to assist you in clarifying your beliefs and prioritizing your values in life. Centered, "together" people find that their personal vision statement enables them to have a solid anchor that can help weather any storm.

> **A PERSONAL VISION STATEMENT ENABLES YOU TO HAVE A SOLID ANCHOR THAT CAN HELP WEATHER ANY STORM.**

My experience working with hundreds of people developing personal visions (individuals from high school students to CEOs) is that this exercise is one of the most important and rewarding things you can do for yourself. It should be a document that you draft with care, refine with pride, and work hard to live by. It should be the very foundation of your belief system. A well-constructed personal vision statement defines:

- Who you are;

- Who and what is important to you;

- What you believe and value most in life; and

- What direction you will take to become the person you are striving to become.

The major problem I have seen with vision statements is that they tend to be *ends* focused, when they should be *means* focused. Your personal vision should state how you live, not what your life produces.

My advice in constructing your statement is to find at least one to two hours that you can devote to this activity. Do it in a somewhat isolated and pleasant environment. Begin the process by listing what you feel are your strengths and weaknesses. Next, list all of the people and things that are important in your life. As you write the statement, keep all of these documents in front of you. Your focus should be to create, at most, a paragraph of about three or four sentences that define

The Contented Achiever

you. Opt for brevity if you can do so without losing meaning. Once you write it and do some preliminary editing, set the statement aside for a few days. Then go back and read it again, making any changes that you feel are needed. This is a very special document. Share it with others.

Below is a sample Personal Vision Statement for your review:

"Life is an adventure - a journey to be enjoyed right now. One of my priorities is to put forth creative energy to enhance the quality of life for myself, family members, associates and clients. I believe that life is valuable and each day is a blessing from God. I make the most of each and every day. I enjoy being centered and focused and always keep promises. My decisions are aligned with my beliefs, and I follow all of my paths wisely."

Your vision statement will play several roles. It will be an emotional smoothing agent. When you find yourself feeling a bit low emotionally or depressed over some temporary "failure" in

YOUR VISION STATEMENT WILL BE AN EMOTIONAL SMOOTHING AGENT AND VALUABLE DECISION TOOL.

your life, pull out your vision statement and read it for a sustainable uplift. Likewise, following a tremendous success or victory, it will serve a grounding role in bringing you back to earth and a more productive reality. In addition to playing

The Contented Achiever

this ongoing balancing role, your vision statement will be a tremendously valuable decision making aid.

I became most impressed with the power of vision or mission statements for organizations when I learned that a major health product manufacturer took an $80 million instant loss based on a reading of its mission statement. Forget customer satisfaction, there was evidence that one of their products had been poisoned and was killing a small number of customers! Management debated the financial aspects of the issue for a few moments, then went into the hallway and read the firm's mission statement crafted by the company's founder in the 1940's. It proclaimed that the firm's primary responsibility was to the doctors, nurses, pharmacists, mothers, fathers and children who either prescribe or consume the organization's products. At that point the decision was clear to pull all the products off the shelf. Today, the product is one of the most trusted and respected brands in the world. What would have been the impact if the mission had focused on ends, such as "maximizing shareholder wealth" (a noble goal but not a mission)? It scares me to think what the outcome would have been.

While the corporate illustration is a powerful and significant example, you can gain similar clarity with a personal statement. I have used my own to make many decisions over the years. I have always been amazed how uncertainty bows to clarity after a quick read of my vision statement. It takes you back to your belief system and moves you away from what are

The Contented Achiever

often distracting short-term issues. Whether it is accepting a job offer, dealing with a client or colleague, or meeting a family challenge, the personal vision statement always helps us stay

> **WRITE, SHARE, REFINE AND USE YOUR VISION STATEMENT AND YOU'LL FIND THAT THE IMPACT ON YOUR LIFE WILL BE DRAMATIC!**

grounded and make solid decisions. Write, share, refine and use your vision statement and you will find that the impact on your life will be dramatic!

Mistaken Certainty and Perfection

Don't try to achieve "certainty" when you write your statement. The desire for certainty could keep you from ever completing it. And although I asked you to describe things as if they were perfect, keep in mind the actual pursuit of perfection is a very unhealthy activity. Go for the constant pursuit of excellence, and leave the pursuit of perfection to the compulsive overachievers of the world. Fritz gave his readers good advice. He told them that if they get stuck with this step JUST MAKE IT UP! You can adjust your statement of desired results or change it anytime you want.

Many people seem to be unhappy or restless because they are unable to make a commitment unless they are certain of everything related to the commitment. That is like the person

The Contented Achiever

who wants to go across town, but waits until all of the traffic lights between one side of town and the other are green. They will always be stuck . . . waiting to make the trip. Life is a series of unplanned stops and detours. None of these can slow you down permanently if you persist and have a clear vision of where you are headed. You will just find another (and sometimes better) way. The fact is, the act of making a commitment is a necessary step for achieving any worthwhile result.

Try making "fluid commitments." That means making a commitment and standing ready to adjust or change it as you discover new information. Flexibility can lead to even better results than you imagined when you began your commitment. When they sent a spaceship to the moon they didn't just fire away, then sit back and hope it got there. The people controlling the flight made a constant series of adjustments with small retro rockets to make sure the spacecraft stayed on track until it reached its target. That's what life is all about. Get started and be willing to make adjustments. The only certainty is that your spacecraft won't reach the moon if you never launch it!

Fine-Tuning Your Vision Statement

- Write your statement as if it is happening now. Describing what you are going to do is not as powerful as describing what you are doing. Actions can only be taken in the present. Choices you make today create your future. Don't worry about the fact that your statement has

The Contented Achiever

arrived at the destination before you and your crew. Act as if you are already there and "magic coincidences" will begin to occur.

- Focus on what you want to happen, not what you do not want to happen.

- Be specific. If you can't write an action plan step to support your desired result, rewrite your desired results and be more specific.

- Keep it brief and simple. It's appropriate to put the statement in bullet point form, outline form or any other format as long as you and anyone else involved understand it.

- Use simple words.

- Make it exciting! If you do not feel some sense of excitement when reading the statement, rewrite it with pizzazz. How many people would have listened if Martin Luther King had boasted, "I have a strategic plan" instead of "I have a dream!" People are moved to action by emotions, not logic. This statement can also be a source of inspiration during challenging times.

Step Two: Current Assessment

Figuring out where you are today sounds like a simple thing to do. Not quite true. It takes a great deal of objectivity and introspection to assess your reality accurately. Think of people you know who have a skewed view of their lives. You might see immediately that their assessment of the situation is less than clear. Do any of the following situations sound familiar?

- Your associate complains that someone less qualified was promoted to vice president, yet you recognize that it was probably your friend's lack of strategic thinking that swayed the choice.

- Your mother worries constantly that she will have no money to retire on, though she and your father have invested wisely and have a perfectly comfortable nest egg.

- Your brother-in-law wonders why his third wife left him when he's such a devoted husband. You and your spouse both know that he shows no interest in either his wife or his children.

It is not unusual for people to be in denial about their reality, which means they don't see themselves or their circumstances as they really are. Nevertheless, objectively evaluating your own situation is an absolutely essential step. And if efficiency and effectiveness are important to you, this step is critical.

Let's turn again to our airplane flight to analyze this step. You're the pilot and you have a clear vision of what you desire to accomplish. You want to fly to Dallas; however, you are not clear about your current reality. You have become confused and momentarily can't remember if you're starting from Phoenix or Seattle. About this time, the fuel truck drives up and the driver asks you how much fuel to load on board for the trip. Let's look at both possibilities.

Scenario 1: You're actually in Phoenix; however, you think you are in Seattle. You will ask for more fuel than you can possibly burn between Phoenix and Dallas. As you approach Dallas, your flight engineer might well tell you that the aircraft is too heavy to land. You will then have to dump fuel in order to bring the aircraft down to the proper landing weight. This results in unnecessary risk and waste.

Scenario 2: You're in Seattle; however, you think you are in Phoenix. You tell the people to load enough fuel for the trip from Phoenix to Dallas and then take off. Somewhere during the trip, mean old Mr. Gravity will show you the error in your thinking.

I think you can see that it is extremely important to have a realistic assessment of your current reality in relation to the results you desire. Otherwise, you may be destined to waste fuel (your own emotional and physical energy) and crash land.

You may want to enlist the help of one or more trusted friends or family members to bounce ideas off and to give you feedback about your reality. Of course, their opinions are only opinions, and are filtered through their own outlook on the

The Contented Achiever

world. But by soliciting feedback from several people, you have a better opportunity to weigh different answers. Feedback can be helpful; just keep it in perspective.

Step Three: Action!

This third component of the Creating Desired Results model is the action plan. Once you have completed steps one and two, this one becomes relatively easy. You know where you are and you know where you want to go. Now develop some specific, measurable steps or actions to get you from where you are to where you want to go. Once again, keep it simple.

Often what to do is more difficult to determine than what to do *next*. Just stay focused on what to do next and be willing to constantly update your plan. At this point, vow to stay in action mode. Remember, the action plan is where "the rubber hits the road." Procrastination can be a disastrous immobilizer here if you let it.

Let's say, for example, you have decided to become an astronaut, and you do not currently have any idea where to start. This would appear to be an overwhelming and perhaps impossible task. You could get sidetracked thinking about how much education you need, how long it will take to get in physical condition, and other things that would be necessary at some point in the future. That's when you might be likely to

The Contented Achiever

say, "Forget it. I'll never be able to do this." Come back from the future, and focus only on the next step. There might be several excellent ones. You could:

- Read a book on astronauts.

- Watch videos on the space program.

- Meet with an astronaut.

- Visit a space museum.

Now, isn't that better? You get the idea. Get started on something that will move you in the direction of your desired results. There is tremendous power in just getting started. It takes a lot of fuel to get an airplane off the ground and to cruising altitude. Once it is in the air, it takes much less fuel to keep the momentum going and the aircraft at level flight.

Double Check Your Vision and Your Plan

Let's address a few more issues regarding the Creating Desired Results model. As you develop your model, make sure you do a good job of reconciling the action plan and the vision steps. Analyze your vision statement and make sure that for everything you say you are going to focus on in the vision statement, you have specific action plan steps. Let's use a business example. Suppose you're developing a vision statement for your department and you state, "We have the best trained employees in the organization," and there is no corresponding step in the action plan to support this desire. You are not finished. There must be a step related to training. For example, "We will develop a sales training class by June 10, and will certify 50% of employees in it by year end." All steps should be specific, connected, observable and measurable.

IF YOU HAVEN'T SPECIFIED HOW YOU WILL ARRIVE AT YOUR GOAL, YOU HAVEN'T COMPLETED THE CYCLE TO CREATE YOUR DESIRED RESULTS.

If you have not specified how you will arrive at your goal, you have not completed the cycle to create your desired results. If you want to stay on track, you have two choices: add a step to the action plan or take the desired result out of your vision statement. Likewise, if you have a step in your action plan that does not relate to anything in your vision statement, delete the action plan step or add the desired result to your vision statement. It is important to reconcile these two steps. The cycle must be completed if you want to avoid failure and frustration.

The Contented Achiever

Does It Matter Where You Start?

We've talked about steps one, two and three, but do you have to start with step one? Some prefer to start with the current assessment component. They want to know where they are before they decide where they are going. Others are more comfortable starting with the vision. Very few people admit that they want to start with the action plan, although surprisingly this is where most people actually jump in.

This process is a cycle, so technically you can start anywhere and achieve your desired results as long as you quickly complete the other two components of the cycle. There will even be certain situations where it makes the most sense to just take immediate action. For example, if someone is lying on the ground bleeding, you don't want to spend much time getting a clear vision of the person in perfect health before you take action. Skip assessing current reality. Stop the bleeding, then complete the cycle.

Despite the fact that you may begin anywhere in the cycle, there are some distinct advantages to starting with the vision. If you start with an assessment of the current reality, you have placed yourself squarely in the middle of your existing limitations. You may eliminate or not think of some good ideas because they seem to be impossible considering your current reality; however, "anything goes" in brainstorming your vision statement.

Are You Still Puzzled?

One good way to evaluate the best place to start is to think of the process as putting together a jigsaw puzzle. We have three options:

- We could simulate the action plan step by opening the puzzle box and randomly trying to put the pieces together. We are taking action.

Mathematically, we could accomplish the desired result, getting the puzzle together, if we kept trying different combinations of pieces. However, it would not be a very efficient way. It would be a rough and time-consuming journey from our current reality to our desired results.

- The second option is to complete a current assessment in the case of the puzzle by examining and grouping all of the puzzle pieces according to some system (edges, color, shape, unique characteristics, etc.).

If we start by doing this, we have significantly increased the odds of getting the puzzle put together more efficiently. Our journey will be much smoother.

- But why not start by picking up the box and looking at the picture on the cover?

This is analogous to creating a mental picture of what it looks like when things are going right. You can see how the pieces

The Contented Achiever

will fit together by study-
ing the relationships of
the objects in the picture
before you take action.
With this clear mental
picture of what you are
trying to accomplish, you
are off to an excellent,

> **A CLEAR MENTAL PICTURE OF WHAT YOU ARE TRYING TO ACCOMPLISH WILL SAVE ONE OF YOUR MOST VALUABLE RESOURCES: TIME.**

highly focused start in a manner that will save you much of
that highly valued resource we call time.

It's a simple, cyclical process with only three components.
Don't be fooled by its simplicity. It is a very powerful model.
In fact, if you consider most of the failures or frustrations in
your life, you'll probably recognize that they were caused by
breaking this cycle. You may not have enough clarity in your
vision statement, you may be in denial about your current
reality or your action plan may not support your vision.

Think of this model as an opportunity to clarify every worthwhile thing you will attempt in your life. Use it to take in a
tremendous number of choices and convert them to specific
actions that will help you create your desired results. It clari-
fies and aligns the choices and actions to help you successfully, effectively and efficiently create your desired results.
Use the model to convert complexity into simplicity, and
thoughts into action.

A Versatile Model

The Creating Desired Results model works in all areas of your life. You can use it to create business results, financial results, relationship results or any other desired results. Try it out with your business by posing some questions.

- Is the leader of your organization as well trained in handling his or her job responsibilities as an airline pilot? Does he have to continually demonstrate that he's highly competent and able to handle the mission? When she's performing her mission, are you convinced that she's mentally and physically engaged in successfully completing it? (When asking this question, members of the board of directors should be focusing on the company CEO, the company CEO should be focusing on the division leaders, division leaders should be focusing on their direct reports and so forth on down the line in the organization. At the individual level, ask yourself all of these questions, since you're the CEO of your life.)

- Does the leader of your organization have a clear, well-articulated vision, a realistic current assessment and a well thought out action plan to accomplish the vision?

- Do all of the people involved in carrying out the mission have the right resources (the proper aircraft in the case of our pilot) to accomplish the job, and are the resources in excellent working order?

The Contented Achiever

- Are the people well trained and mentally engaged in the task at hand? Do they understand where their "flight" is headed and know what their part is in successfully completing the vision?

- Do the customers (passengers) desire to go where the organization is planning to take them? I won't spend much time on this issue, but the product development and marketing experts should make sure this element exists if they want the organization to survive in the long run.

- Are the stakes for the passengers and the leaders of the organization similar? Granted, the cost of failure in most organizations is not the same as the cost of failure on an airplane. However, the use of incentives such as stock options and grants are currently a popular way to align the interest of the leaders of an organization with the interest of the customers and shareholders. Put another way, how much differently would the organization be run if the cost of success or failure was the same for all parties?

Flying High

In the example of our airline flight, the Creating Desired Results model can be used to assure that all the "bases are covered" before you get on the airplane. By closing the Creating Desired Results cycle on pilot training, crew training, aircraft maintenance, fuel requirements and all other aspects of flying an airplane, you can sit on the airplane and feel confident that you will have a successful flight. Why would you accept any less in creating the desired results of your life? Begin your journey today and use the Creating Desired Results model to convert your thoughts and dreams into action and results.

POINTS TO PONDER

★ Do you have a clear vision of what you desire to accomplish with your life?

★ Are you willing to make the commitments necessary to achieve this vision?

★ Have you completed an accurate current assessment?

★ Do you have an action plan that will move you from your current reality to your vision?

★ Have you reconciled your action plan with your desired results?

★ Are you flexible enough to adjust your plan as new situations occur and new information is available?

"ONE CANNOT DIRECTLY CHOOSE HIS
CIRCUMSTANCES, BUT HE CAN CHOOSE
HIS THOUGHTS, AND SO INDIRECTLY, YET
SURELY, SHAPE HIS CIRCUMSTANCES."
JAMES ALLEN

The Contented Achiever

Chapter Three
The Impact of Thoughts, Words and Actions on Your Circumstances: Getting From There to Here

Paul Harvey tells a story of a young artist who had just been engaged to paint a portrait of a local builder. The artist was so excited, feeling so good, since it was his first major commission. He went down to his favorite little sidewalk cafe to enjoy a glass of wine and celebrate the portrait he was to paint. While he was sitting there sipping his wine, he looked over and saw a newspaper lying in a chair at the next table. At the top of the front page in bold print were the words "Hard Times Are Coming." The more he looked at it, the more uptight and worried he became.

The restaurant owner came by in a moment and said, "Shall I get you another glass of wine or something to eat?" "No," he said, "Just bring me my check. I must go right now." The

The Contented Achiever

owner replied, "Is something wrong?" The artist said, "Hard times are coming, and this is no time for me to be frivolously spending my time and money. I must get to work."

The artist left, and the restaurant owner began thinking, "Hard times are coming?" And the more he thought about it, the more uptight and worried he became. He picked up the telephone and called his wife and said, "Sweetheart, that new dress you ordered for the annual banquet is awfully expensive for something that you are only going to wear once. I believe hard times are coming, and maybe you should call them and put off the dress for now."

She reluctantly said, "Well, all right." So she called the local dress shop and said, "I know you've already ordered the material for my beautiful new dress, but my husband said that hard times are coming and we need to pull in our purse strings and be more frugal. I'm going to have to cancel the dress."

The proprietor said, "Well, I certainly hate to hear that but I understand." The dress shop owner began thinking about it and the more she thought about it, the more uptight and worried she became. She called her local builder and said, "I understand that hard times are coming. It's a bad time for me to be doubling the size of my dress shop. I can't take on that type of obligation right now."

The builder thought about what she had said. And he picked

The Contented Achiever

up the phone and called the young artist. He said, "Hard times are coming and this is no time for me to be spending money on a portrait. I'm going to have to cancel it."

The young artist understood. It was just what he had anticipated. Feeling rejected and sorrowful, he went to the sidewalk cafe to drown his sorrows in a bottle of wine. As he sat there drinking he looked over in the chair about 10 feet away. There was the newspaper with the headline that said, "Hard Times Are Coming." He walked over, picked it up and examined it very closely. The dateline was ten years old. Someone had left the old paper there when they were unpacking dishes for the restaurant. The thought that the headline conveyed had infected the thinking of many leaders of the community. They began preparing for the worst for no real reason at all, except that they let their unfounded negativity create an undesired reality.

The Effect of Thoughts, Words and Actions on Your Future

The preceding story is about the power of thoughts in your life, and how thoughts, words and actions bring the reality of your mental world into your physical world. Thoughts, words and actions are like powerful magnets that attract the circumstances of your life.

To create the future that you desire, you must start by developing the habit of controlling what you think. Thoughts are the ancestors of all actions, so nothing can be created in *your* life unless *you* think of it first.

> **YOUR GREATEST RETURN ON EFFORT COMES FROM LEARNING TO CONTROL YOUR THOUGHTS.**

Nothing can be created, period, unless someone thinks of it first. Your thoughts are not only the root cause of any problems you may be experiencing, they are also the root cause of any successes you are enjoying. Your greatest return on effort comes from learning to control your thoughts.

We live in a society where others are constantly trying to take control of our thinking. Bosses, friends, co-workers, spouses, family members and others are constantly trying to get us to think like they want us to think. Surprisingly enough, they are very successful much of the time, because we allow it.

Companies spend vast amounts of money to produce advertising and public relations that will influence our thinking. You may have heard the saying, "People often buy things they don't need with money they don't have to impress people they don't like." Sad, but often true. Buying unnecessary things may or may not result in a problem for you, but doing unnecessary things just because others want you to can have a significant influence on your life.

The Contented Achiever

My Son, the Doctor

Consider how many people make a career decision based on someone else's thoughts about what they should do. Picking a career is one of the most important decisions that you will make in your life, yet very few people make a conscious decision to select a career. Their career choice just happens. They disregard their own passions and let the economy, parents, friends or other outside influences select for them. They choose by default.

Even the process of getting a college education actually encourages this. You are the student and you should be using your time in college to develop your true gifts and talents in order to get you where you want to go in life. But other people are calling most of the shots. In fact, your entire college education is almost totally designed to meet someone else's needs. The faculty, committees, government officials, potential employers and others design your educational path in a manner that will meet their needs. Therefore, most people take courses by default and usually take the minimum number of courses required to meet everyone else's needs and never get around to the courses that support their passions.

Perhaps that's why, in mid-career, many people begin to question the choice they made. Even people who are highly successful often begin having second thoughts. So, how did you come by your profession? Are you in a career that was chosen by default? If you have a business degree, would you choose more liberal arts courses if you had it to do over? Or vice versa? Is your career well aligned with your true passion? If not, why not?

You see how your thoughts years ago -- or lack thereof -- created the situation you're in today. The less centered we are in our decision-making processes, the more susceptible we are to the attitudes, influences, and assertions of others.

A career is only one example of the elements of your life that you can and should control. Not by thinking of it in its macro sense, "My Life," but in terms of the small choices that joined hands to put you where you are, and that will join hands to put you somewhere in the future.

Chain Reactions

A physicist being interviewed by a National Public Radio reporter used an interesting analogy to explain the importance and benefits of breaking things down into simpler elements.

He broke down a library as follows:

-Libraries are made up of . . .
-Books, which are made up of . . .
-Chapters, which are made up of . . .

The Contented Achiever

-Paragraphs, which are made up of . . .

-Sentences, which are made up of . . .

-Words, which are made up of . . .

-Letters, which can be created on a computer using . . .

-A programming language consisting of "ones" and "zeros"

In its simplest form, you could create a library by using "ones" and "zeros."

Physicists use the same method to understand the almost incomprehensible and vast universe that we live in. The more they can break the universe down into its simplest elements, the more they understand it, and the easier it is to control the forces of the universe that affect us. Understanding molecules, atoms, protons, neutrons, electrons, quarks and other quantum particles has significantly increased mankind's ability to understand and control our universe. Like the physicist, we can dramatically increase our ability to control our future by understanding how to control the simplest elements involved in creating our future: our thoughts.

Now You See It . . .

The phenomenon that is set in motion by splitting the atom and starting a nuclear chain reaction is not significantly different from the phenomenal chain reaction that was described

The Contented Achiever

in the story about the young artist. How could he have changed the outcome of the story? He could have tried to change the actions of each of the people involved in the story, which seems like (and is) an impossible task. Overwhelming and daunting. But return to the beginning of the story, and imagine the different outcome if the artist had not been so influenced by those four little words: Hard Times Are Coming. It was merely type on a page until his runaway thoughts based on unjustified fear made the idea real.

> BY LEARNING TO ACCEPT, ADJUST OR CHANGE OUR THOUGHTS IN THE PRESENT, WE GAIN THE ABILITY TO CHANGE OUR FUTURE.

So, what did he have to control to change his future? Only his thoughts at the time he read the headline. We can further simplify the task of creating the future we desire by understanding that we only need to control our thoughts in the present moment. By learning to accept, adjust or change our thoughts in the present, we gain the ability to change our future.

Although you can mentally create the illusion that you are in the past or in the future, unless you've created a time machine, you can never be there physically. When you try to think about your future right now, you can only think of it as a series of probable outcomes. Life offers an endless selection of choices, or forks in the road. You may constantly pass these forks with little thought where one road or the other will take you. As in the case of getting a college education, we often let

The Contented Achiever

others choose our path, rather than choosing it ourselves. Look back on your life and you can undoubtedly identify people you met, books you read, things you heard or experiences that had a significant positive or negative influence on your future. When you were young, your future could have easily been influenced by an encouraging teacher, an abusive parent, a touchdown made, a pass dropped, a book read or test failed. All of these experiences generated thoughts on your part at the time they occurred and helped shape the person you are now.

If you can improve your ability to control your thoughts in the present moment, you can improve your ability to create your future life circumstances. Thoughts in the present moment drive how you feel, what you say and what you do.

Herding Cats and Other Impossible Activities

The concept of controlling thoughts may sound like trying to herd a thousand cats; it seems like it just can't be done. We live in a world of sensory overload often resulting in near chaos. Things happen fast, and we're expected to operate at a fast pace. In business, our boss, our co-workers, our subordinates, our customers, our phone, our fax machine, our e-mail and many other forces pull us in every direction. We are expected to produce significant sales and earnings growth and, at the same time, downsize our support staff and reduce our use of company resources. We are continuously asked to do more with less. We must do all this and be "Cosby-like" parents and spouses, true-blue friends and pillars of the community. Thoughts constantly race through our minds. We often feel as if we never have enough time to think of anything for more than a few seconds. Life has become so complex that understanding it is like a physicist trying to understand how the universe works. Aha!

Maybe we need to continue to break things down into simpler elements. You may have already learned that you can gain better control over your life by breaking everything down into a day. Some call this "time management." You plan on a daily basis, establish daily routines and use day-timers to control your daily activities.

If you operate with a daily plan, you are probably more successful than those who do not; however, in a world that operates at ultra-high speed, you may find that this method is no longer sufficient. Things that previously took days are now expected in minutes. You come into work with a well thought out plan but you never get started on it. A crisis disrupts your plan early in the day and you never get back on track. You can only herd 3 of the 1000 cats and 997 are running wildly about. When this occurs and the old method no longer works, it is time to look for a simpler element to control.

The Myth of Time Management

If you have been trying to control your life through time management, brace yourself: You cannot control time; it passes at its own pace no matter what your desires or intentions. It is,

YOU CANNOT MANAGE TIME. YOU CAN ONLY MANAGE YOUR ACTIVITIES OR ACTIONS THAT CONSUME TIME AS IT PASSES.

therefore, more logical to break your day down into something you can control -- your own activities.

In chapter one, we discussed a concept that will help you develop healthy long-term thinking patterns by clearly defining your concept of success. In chapter two, we shortened our time frame and discussed a model that will help you with intermediate-term success. Now we are down to an element that is critical to your success, because long-term and intermediate-term success are simply functions of how well you control daily activity elements. In other words, the here and now.

Thinking of your day in terms of "activity management" rather than "time management" will improve your ability to create the life that you desire. You just cannot manage time. You can only manage activities or actions that consume time as it passes. A similar dilemma happens to people who become very goal oriented, putting a lot of time and effort into developing written goals that are not backed up or supported by action. You cannot "do a goal;" you can only "do an action." Goal setting is ineffective if it is not backed up by meaningful and appropriate action. Focus on investing your time rather than just spending it. Some business leaders think that they have completed a strategic plan when they develop a set of worthy sounding goals such as, "We will earn $100 million next year," or, "We will produce gross sales of $750 million next year." Statements alone will not get anything done. They must be backed up by specific and meaningful action.

Remember when we talked about the NASA scientists sending a rocket to the moon? Daily activity elements are like retro-rockets. After launching the main rocket, the NASA experts fire a series of small retro-rockets to make small adjustments to the flight path and keep the rocket on the proper course. Once you establish your overall intent, the desired results that you have defined as success, you must then become keenly aware of the daily activities that are necessary to keep you on the right course. You create what you desire one step at a time. Nothing seems as difficult or complex if you think of it in terms of the most appropriate next step.

The Pause that Refreshes

When you divide your day into activity elements, you also create natural opportunities to pause and reflect on what you

The Contented Achiever

intend to do next. Your segments may include simple, routine activities such as getting ready to go to work, driving your car, watching your child sleep, or enjoying a meal. They may be more complex, such as completing the next step of a major project or preparing a speech. As you consider the segments you are going to include in your day, remember: If you have chosen to do it, it must be important because you are exchanging something very valuable for it -- your time.

> **"BE ALWAYS RESOLUTE WITH THE PRESENT HOUR. EVERY MOMENT IS OF INFINITE VALUE; FOR IT IS THE REPRESENTATIVE OF ETERNITY."**
> JOHANN WOLFGANG VON GOETHE

Before beginning an activity, pause and think about your specific intent. What are you going to do next? Why are you doing this? Is this action supporting the life you intend to create? Is it giving you a proper return on your time investment?

Say, for example, you intend to live a balanced life. Is this next action going to support your financial goals, intellectual goals, relationship goals, recreational goals, or other goals that you have determined to be important for creating a balanced life? If, during the pause, you cannot easily connect your action to one of your goals, reconsider your action. If, during the pause, you think about it and you are still confused about the desirability of your next action, read on.

The Contented Achiever

Let Emotions Be Your Guide

In chapter two, we discussed how to reconcile your vision and action plan. You learned that your action plan should include specific, measurable activities that clearly support your overall vision. But how can you be sure that the activities you have chosen are the right ones for you? This is, in effect, one of the most important questions that you can ask. It is an extremely personal question that no one else can answer for you. It gets to the heart of your curiosity about life in general. It is asked in many different ways. What is my purpose in life? What am I supposed to be doing? What is my contribution?

In order to answer these questions, you must realize that you have constant access to very effective internal guides which can serve as an internal lighthouse. The guides are with you 24 hours a day, 365 days a year. These guides are your emotions. Some people may advise you not to be emotional or not to allow your emotions to be your guide. They may advise you to let logic be your guide. Guess what -- you rarely have a choice. In the end, at the last moment before a decision is made, emotions almost always take over. People, for the most part, are driven by emotions, not logic. Think of the big decisions in life such as getting married, buying a house, or a car. You may employ logical thinking to get you to the edge of the decision-making process; however, emotions are usually what push you over the edge to your final decision. Logic can only take you so far in the decision making process. Logic should

The Contented Achiever

not be discounted or discarded . . . but a rich, meaningful life is based largely on emotions and passion.

Emotions have many names. You know them as joy, happiness, contentment, serenity, focus, clarity, frustration, sadness, sorrow, restlessness, guilt, confusion and many others. If you break them down into their simplest elements, there are only two categories of these internal guides. One guide sends you positive internal messages and the other sends you negative internal messages.

Having said this, we will now share with you one of the secrets of creating a successful, meaningful life. Are you ready for this secret? If you get this point, life will immediately begin to improve and you will be on your way to creating the life you desire. The point is:

INVEST YOUR TIME ON DAILY ACTIVITIES THAT CREATE POSITIVE INTERNAL EMOTIONS!

I know it seems too simple, but you must constantly be aware of how your emotions are responding to your thoughts, words and actions. You must be accountable for your own thinking process, disciplining yourself to reject potentially ill-fated external thoughts. If you feel bad, (call it guilt, frustration, confusion or whatever), change what you are thinking about. When you do this effectively, what you are saying and doing will follow the lead.

The Contented Achiever

Remember that it is normal for negative emotions to emerge in difficult situations. An example would be a salesperson who has been rejected. In such a situation, it is important to identify the real source of your negative feelings. A negative reaction to another person's comments often indicates that we are attaching more importance to their opinion than our own. However, the real source of the negative feeling may be related to your self-esteem, personal beliefs or lack of confidence. In such cases, be sure you turn these negative emotions into positive emotions by addressing the true source of the problem. Rejection doesn't mean you need to get out of sales. It may simply mean the customer can't make a decision, won't make a decision, that you need to improve your selling skills or many other things. Understand the real source of negative emotions and work to convert them to positive emotions. Be accountable for both your conclusions and responses. Knee-jerk reactions seldom pay dividends.

Snowballs Are Made Up of Snowflakes

Emotions can give you feedback on which thoughts to nurture and which thoughts to discard, but then you encounter another challenge. How can you change your thoughts? Sometimes you feel as if you have no control over them. They seem to be like an avalanche rolling down a hill, picking up speed, gaining momentum and unstoppable. Your thoughts begin to overwhelm you and make you feel as if you are losing control

The Contented Achiever

of your circumstances. You may feel as if you are losing touch with reality or blowing things out of proportion without sound cause, both of which are counterproductive to progress.

But go back to the beginning of the avalanche. It all starts with a few tiny snowflakes. Snowflakes turn into snowballs. Snowballs turn into avalanches. Stopping thoughts when they are like snowflakes is much easier than trying to stop an avalanche of thoughts. If your emotions are at the point where they are sending you a blizzard of negative messages, you are already in trouble. So, the key to controlling your thoughts is to catch them in the snowflake stage and deal with them. As a few negative snowflake-thoughts begin to fall in your life, pause and carefully consider your response. Remember, it is not what happens to you that is important, it is how you respond to what happens to you that really matters.

Here's one example of how a thought can create a positive or a negative avalanche. Suppose a co-worker tells Keith that he overheard the boss saying that Keith is doing a lousy job. Keith might have a sequence of thoughts:

-I'm a stupid idiot.
-I feel so humiliated.
-I'm going to be fired.
-Everyone will know I'm a failure.
-I'll never find another job with this bad recommendation.
-I'll lose my house.

The Contented Achiever

-My wife will leave me.

-I won't be able to educate my children.

And so on.

In such an avalanche of bad thoughts, Keith would be un-likely to make a sane decision about his next steps. He might leave work with a migraine and a sick stomach, scream at the kids, spend the entire night thrashing about, keep his spouse awake, and the next morning start updating his resume and looking for a job before the boss could fire him. All of that from a simple comment that may or may not even be true.

How could things have gone differently if Keith had controlled his thoughts? The co-worker says he heard the boss saying Keith is doing a lousy job. Keith has some thoughts:

-This feels terrible.

-What's the next thing I should do?

-I should approach my boss and find out if it's true.

-I will deal with this confidently and maturely.

-I wonder what I'm supposed to be learning from this?

While Keith couldn't control what his co-worker said, or what his boss did or didn't think, he could control his own thoughts. He could deal with the immediate need to find out whether the statement was true, without jumping ahead to the conse-quences. If the remark was true, then he could explore solu-

The Contented Achiever

tions, but why waste energy on something that is only potentially negative?

In the first situation, Keith made himself utterly miserable before he even knew whether the remark was true. In the second situation, the circumstances did not change; his reaction did. He didn't jump to conclusions or get ten steps ahead of reality. He stayed in the moment, and determined only the next necessary step. By controlling his thoughts, Keith avoided an avalanche that might have resulted, at best, in a headache, and, at worst, in some impulsive and destructive action. Centered people find the right balance of emotion and logic which adds to the quality of their thoughts and actions.

People who are centered and in control of their lives analyze circumstances, pause and think before they respond, deal with the negatives of life when they are in snowflake form and never let them turn into a snowball or avalanche. They, in effect, fire a small retro-rocket, make the necessary adjust-

> **PEOPLE WHO ARE CENTERED DON'T LET SMALL NEGATIVE THOUGHTS TURN INTO BIG NEGATIVE CIRCUMSTANCES.**

ment, and move on with their life. They quickly get back on course. People who are centered in life don't let small negative thoughts turn into big negative circumstances.

The Contented Achiever

> **"THERE IS NOTHING SO WRETCHED OR FOOLISH AS TO ANTICIPATE MISFORTUNES. WHAT MADNESS IS IT IN EXPECTING EVIL BEFORE IT ARRIVES."**
> LUCIUS ANNAEUS SENECA

From There to Here

Most people in life seem to be trying to get from "here to there." They may not know where "there" is, but they feel they will be happy, peaceful, grounded, centered and successful when they get "there" someday. An important principle to keep in mind is . . . regrets keep you in the past and desires keep you in the future. Truly successful and grounded people live in the moment. They do this by understanding the power of thoughts on their circumstances. Their passions in life always reside in the present. They know that the way to fulfill their purpose in life, and to live a successful life is to get not from here to there, but from there to here. "Here" is being in the present moment in control of their thoughts. These people are calm and centered because they have confidently chosen to believe that "Good Times Are Coming!"

The Lessons

What can you learn from this chapter that will help you create the future that you desire?

- You can learn to pay attention to what you are thinking about. You are where you are today because of thoughts

The Contented Achiever

you had in the past. You will create your future with your present thoughts.

- Be sensitive to your emotions. Remember that positive, joyful emotions are telling you that you are on the right track and in alignment with your true purpose in life. Negative emotions are sending you a signal to make a change. It is easier to change negative emotions when they first begin. Confusion is telling you to break the subject of your thoughts into more basic elements.

- Fill your day with activities that will allow you to enjoy the present moment and help you create the life that you desire. Pause before beginning each activity and clarify your intent. Spend time on activities that create positive internal emotions.

- Let your words always support your positive intent. Words can also tell you much about what is really going on in your thoughts. Listen to yourself. For example, do you spend more time talking about what you don't want to happen or what you want to happen? It is imperative that we do the latter.

- When your thoughts, words and actions are in alignment and in support of your intent in the present moment, your future is largely in your control. Get in the habit of controlling what you think, say and do in the present moment.

One of the best techniques for accomplishing everything that we have discussed in this chapter is outlined in Julia

Cameron's book *The Artist's Way*. She suggests that you try a process called morning pages. You hand write three pages of whatever happens to be on your mind every morning. The process is very simple and LIFE CHANGING. I would consider this book homework for people who want to take control of their thoughts and create the life they were meant to live. I have seen it change people's lives within a few days.

POINTS TO PONDER

✖ Are your thoughts, words and actions in alignment with the life you desire to create?

✖ Are you tuned-in to your internal emotional guides?

✖ Are you spending your time on activities that create positive internal emotions?

✖ Are you overly concerned with getting from "here to there"?

✖ Are you investing adequate time in fully understanding and appreciating the here and now?

**WE MAKE THE WORLD WE LIVE IN AND
SHAPE OUR OWN ENVIRONMENT.**
ORISON SWETT MARDEN

The Contented Achiever

4

Chapter Four
Reflecting on Your Belief System

When I was growing up, my father's job often required him to travel four or five days in a week. I occasionally felt sad that we didn't get to spend much time together, but we both looked forward to the few times when we could be together. Most of our "quality time" centered on the two most important things in my life: scouting and stamp collecting. Scouting took us back to nature. Stamp collecting and our imagination took us around the world.

Stamps were my imaginary connection to distant places and times. I may not have been there, but the stamp had been there and I had the stamp. Geography came alive for me, because when I held the stamp, I was holding another piece of the world. I still remember the names of many far away countries that most people don't even know exist.

Once each summer my dad would let me join him on a business trip. We would drive from Kansas City, across his territory to the Colorado line. I would look forward to the trip for months. Dad would let me use his AAA guidebook to pick our stops. I would only consider a motel with a swimming pool, and if the pool had a slide and a diving board, that's definitely where we would stay!

On one trip, Dad had planned a special treat. He had scouted out a great stamp collector's store in downtown Goodland, Kansas. He told me we could stop by and check it out before we headed down the road to Dodge City. I had saved a little money and Dad told me that if I found some stamps that I liked that exceeded my budget, he might even help me swing the deal.

As we headed into the small, musty stamp store, I couldn't believe what I saw. I was in "stamp collector's heaven." The store was absolutely loaded with exciting treasures. As the fighter pilots say, it was a "target rich environment." I was focused, a man on a mission, and it didn't take me long to lock on some targets. After making a case for several items that were well outside my budget, we settled on a 1958 plateblock that we both considered a real find. With all my dollars and a few of Dad's, we completed the mission, got back

The Contented Achiever

in the car and headed down the road to Dodge City with our prized possessions.

At that moment, he was the greatest dad in the world and I was the greatest stamp collector. Life was good!

The stamps were in a protective wax paper sleeve, and (despite Dad's instructions) after we rode for about forty-five minutes, I couldn't stand it a minute longer. I took out the stamps to look at them again. As I pulled them out I was shocked! Behind our plateblock was a hidden one, much rarer than the one we had bought, and surely worth much more.

"Dad, look what I found!" I said. "There's a second set of stamps."

At first he scolded me for taking the stamps out of the sleeve, but then he pulled the car over to take a closer look. I knew at that moment that telling Dad had been a huge mistake.

Dad had one overriding character trait . . . he was brutally honest! The son of a minister, he had no gray areas in life. The world to Dad was strictly black and white. The minute he realized that we had two plateblocks instead of one, he turned the car around and headed back to Goodland.

I pleaded with him, trying every excuse I could think of to convince him that we should keep the extra stamps.

"Dad, look at the times we've paid too much for stamps. This just evens things out."

"Dad, the storeowner probably didn't pay for them either. I'll bet he didn't even know they were there."

I shifted to more desperate measures. "Dad, we will miss our pool time together."

Nothing phased him. We were headed back to the stamp store. Right then, he was the worst dad in the world.

As we walked back into the store, the owner gave us a strange look. Dad said, "My son has something to tell you." The storeowner glared at me. I felt awful and ashamed, even though I hadn't done anything wrong. The storeowner made the mistake, not me. This wasn't fair.

Reluctantly, I told him about the extra stamps. He scowled at me. I couldn't believe it. He actually scowled at me! This ungrateful fool didn't even say thanks. He didn't offer me a reward. He just grabbed the stamps out of my hand. Now I knew we should have kept the stamps! Dad was wrong. He was wrong, wrong, wrong!

As we drove off, I launched a long-winded attack on the storeowner. "Dad, can you believe that guy? We should have never returned the stamps. He was a jerk. He didn't even

The Contented Achiever

seem to care. He didn't deserve to get the stamps back. We should have never done that for him."

Dad had one simple response. "Son, we didn't do anything for him. We did it for us."

That was almost 40 years ago. Dad was a wonderful man who lived his life with dignity and died with grace. Although I often didn't understand him, as I get older, he continues to seem smarter. He taught me how to treat people, how to develop character and the basic beliefs necessary to live a successful life. His beliefs are alive and well in me, in my children, and in many other people that he touched during his lifetime. Dad, I miss you. I do understand. And by the way, I love you, and I thank you, more for the intangible gifts than anything tangible you ever gave me.

Corrective Lens

When I reflect on my personal belief system, it's obvious that I needed the "corrective lens" that my Dad provided on the road to Dodge City years ago. I was not seeing clearly. Not only was I blurring the lines between right and wrong, I had lost sight of who was the true beneficiary of honesty. Why do I remember this story so vividly? Why did this experience make an impression on me that will go with me to my grave? Why did this lesson in the past have such a powerful influence on the person that I am today? It's because my dad understood the value of a sound belief system and he understood the power of a "teachable moment."

He probably wanted to go on to the pool just like I did. He knew it was not a big deal financially for the storeowner, but he knew it was a huge deal in terms of the development of my belief system and my character. This was one of those times when he could teach me a lesson that I would never forget, not by telling, but by doing and showing. His thoughts, words and actions were in total harmony with his beliefs.

A poem best describes what happened between me and my dad on that day in Kansas:

The Sermon

I'd rather see a sermon, than hear one any day.
I'd rather you walk with me, than merely show the way.
For the lessons you deliver may be very wise and true.
But I think I'll get my lessons by observing what you do.
I might misunderstand, all the high advice you give.
But I won't misunderstand, how you act and how you live.
                                        Edgar Guest

On that day in Kansas, I saw a sermon that I will never forget.

One of the critical characteristics of a person who enjoys peace of mind is the ability to remain anchored to their belief system when the world around them may be in total chaos.

The Contented Achiever

What's in the Well Comes Up in the Bucket

You might think that by the time you're grown, your beliefs are set and there's no more work to do in that regard. Oh, but there is, for several reasons:

- Some of your beliefs are helping you and you need to reinforce them.

- Some of your beliefs are hurting you and you need to change them.

- Some of your beliefs have fallen by the way, and you need to remind yourself of them.

I was fortunate to have a loving father who taught me some healthy lessons. Not everyone is as lucky. Nevertheless, we have all had our days in Kansas, times in our lives that shaped our current beliefs and resulting behaviors, for better or worse.

> OUR BELIEF SYSTEM IS ANOTHER OF THOSE POWERFUL INTANGIBLES WE MUST NUTURE AND CARE FOR.

When we become adults, we may not have loving parents to mirror our behavior, or to show us where we deviate from our belief systems. In fact, as adults, only we can decide what goals we want, and where we want our lives to take us. We must rely upon ourselves to recognize our own teachable moments, and to prescribe the necessary corrective lens. That requires some looking inward, because, like your emotions, your belief system is an invisible guide. It doesn't matter whether or not you are aware that your belief system is guiding your actions. It is there, in the shadows, doing its work. It is guiding everything you think, say and do.

Since people cannot see their belief system, sometimes they never get around to sufficiently examining their beliefs. Their by-line of life seems to be, "Let the chips fall where they may." They put very little time and effort into improving, refining and changing their beliefs. They do not make it a priority to consciously become aware of their beliefs. Trust me, it is a very good use of your time. Our belief system is another of those powerful intangibles we must nurture and care for.

The process of reflecting on your belief system includes the three approaches we talked about in the introduction:

- Awareness of your belief system.

- Understanding your belief system.

- Applying the knowledge of your belief system to your life.

By looking carefully at what beliefs are exhibiting themselves in our lives and by seeing how our beliefs line up with our

The Contented Achiever

goals, we can begin to align our thinking to accomplish what our hearts desire.

Helpful and Unhelpful Beliefs

Besides, "Honesty is the best policy," which clearly has heavy meaning for me, what are some beliefs that drive people's lives? Here are some examples of beliefs some people hold, some more easily recognized than others, some valid and some in-valid:

-You must give an honest day's work for a day's pay.
-You must only do what it takes to get by.
-All people are created equal.
-You can do anything you set your mind to.
-You are not worthy of success.
-Early to bed and early to rise makes a man healthy, wealthy and wise.
-Never say nice things about yourself. A braggart is obnoxious.
-You have to work more than eight hours a day to get ahead.
-A woman's place is in the home.
-Voting is an important responsibility, as well as a right.

And so on. Let's just take one of the statements and see how it could affect you positively or negatively. Try "You have to work more than eight hours a day to get ahead." If this is part of your belief system, it might manifest itself in your life in several ways:

- You might become extremely successful financially by pouring all your energy into your work.

- You might become a workaholic, because you believe the quality of your work is measured by the quantity.

- You might never develop a healthy relationship, because you might never be willing to spend adequate time with another person.

- You could be overwhelmed by the concept of working more than eight hours a day, and just give up.

- You could ruin your health by not relaxing enough.

Depending upon what your goals are, any of these might help or hurt you. If, for instance, your goal is to have a balanced life, then becoming a workaholic would certainly not help you achieve it. Your belief -- you must work more than eight hours a day to get ahead -- would probably be standing in your way.

We all have both helpful and harmful beliefs about ourselves and others, and about how people should live. Our goal in this chapter is to try to increase the helpful ones, and decrease the harmful ones.

The Contented Achiever

Step One: Awareness of Your Beliefs

The first step is to figure out what your core beliefs are, and where they pop up in your life.

We've already determined that they are invisible. So, how can you see your beliefs? It is really no different from the way you can see electricity: You see the result. Try to explain electricity to most people and you will be met with a dull blank stare. "Huh?" they will say. However, these same people have no trouble seeing the result of whatever electricity is when you flip on a light switch. It's simple: Electricity is the thing that makes the lights come on. You still may have a hard time mentally grasping the concept of electricity, but you believe in it because you pay the light bill.

Like electricity, and like the poem about the living sermon, you can see people's beliefs by observing the outward results. By seeing the outward results of people's lives and knowing that these results are driven by their inner beliefs, you can begin to understand the power of a person's belief system. Understand a person's belief system and you understand the person. The ability to do this will help you with practical matters such as making the next sale or with more important matters such as not letting someone else's beliefs and actions affect your sense of inner peace.

Step Two: Understanding Your Beliefs

Now, let's get personal. This book is primarily to help you see clearly. Let's talk about your beliefs. Although most of us spend the majority of our lives looking outside ourselves and trying to figure out why other people do what they do, we often devote little time to examining our own beliefs.

- Why do we believe what we believe?

- Why do we fold our socks and underwear the way we do?

- Why do we buy the brands that we buy?

- Why do we take jobs that we don't enjoy?

- Why do we respond to criticism the way we do?

> YOU BECAME THE PERSON YOU ARE TODAY BECAUSE OF THE PEOPLE YOU MET, THE LESSONS YOU LEARNED, AND THE EXPERIENCES THAT YOU HAVE HAD.

The best way to discover where your beliefs come from is to map out your life from the earliest time you can remember to the present, and look for forks in the road. Pay special attention to the times you took the unexpected fork in the road. The times when you changed your mind and replaced an old belief with

The Contented Achiever

a new belief. You became the person you are today because of the people you met, the lessons you learned, and the experiences that you have had. Take some time to inventory these people, lessons and experiences. They can impact your belief system and how you live your life, so don't take them lightly.

Write down your "changepoints" in life. Times when you took a fork in the road that sent you in a new direction. When I first did this exercise, I was surprised that some experiences that seemed so insignificant at the time ended up sending my life in a totally different direction. For example, one of my sister's boyfriends took the time to show me his guitar and a few guitar chords. That brief encounter resulted in a lifetime enjoyable passion for me. An economics class field trip resulted in a major career decision that would influence every working day of my life. My high school friend's dad, an airline captain, offered to take me flying and I have not lost interest in aviation since. A tiny book that I read over twenty years ago has fueled a lifetime journey to learn about life.

Take a break from reading, find a quiet place and map out your path to the person you are today.

Checking and Challenging Your Beliefs

The key question to ask yourself now is: Are my beliefs getting me where I want to go? Are they on my side or in my way?

Since you're reading this book, there might well be something in your life that needs to be fine-tuned. It could be your career, a relationship, or your spiritual life. You may be less than satisfied with any number of areas. It is often the case that your belief system is simultaneously part of the problem and part of the solution. The following ideas will help you gain clarification.

If you wonder which beliefs are hindering your progress, look for sources of frustration, confusion or negativity in your life, and follow the map of your life backwards to any underlying belief that could have created that circumstance. To do this, consider the most significant positive and negative events in your life and retrospectively evaluate the beliefs and decisions that caused their occurrence. The more you think about this, the more information will emerge to consider.

Since we are all creatures of habit, it is human nature to cling to old beliefs, even when they are undermining our dreams. The passage of time often makes old beliefs sacred. We have all encountered the "that's the way we have always done it" people.

Letting go of old beliefs can be painful. But, like a trapeze artist, if you never let go, you can never get to the other side. You will never move to the next level in life.

Challenging old beliefs serves another useful purpose. The

  The Contented Achiever

process will cause you to re-commit to those beliefs and values that you know you should continue honoring, more aware than ever that they have served you well.

Faith and the Farmer

The five senses can only take you so far in life. At some point we must all examine the concept of faith. Whether you associate faith with religion or not, in this context we're talking about believing in something you can't see. Perhaps you might also call this trust.

Since in the present moment you, in effect, only believe what you already know, you must understand and rely on faith to develop new beliefs that will take you to greater heights. Faith is the pathway to the next level, whatever that may be for you. And as long as you are a human on this earth, there is always a next level.

"NOW FAITH IS THE SUBSTANCE OF THINGS HOPED FOR, THE EVIDENCE OF THINGS NOT SEEN."
HEBREWS, CHAPTER 11, VERSE 1

Trusting things not seen is one of the most difficult challenges of life. It requires a thorough understanding of the concept of faith. One of the best ways to understand the concept of faith is to think like a farmer. Imagine that you are a farmer who has just completed the planting cycle. You stand at the edge of your farm and you survey your fields. Right now, you see little tangible results of your efforts. You have invested heavily in farm equipment, seed, fertilizer, as well as your time. You see nothing but plowed ground -- dirt. But you know that something unseen is going on underground. You also know that if you continue to nurture the fields, something will appear with the passage of time. Faith is simply the process that is going on in your mind between the moment that you complete planting until the first plant breaks through the surface of your field. Faith requires patience, and trust in the unseen forces that turn seeds into plants.

You are the farmer of the field called your life. You must plant new seeds, quality seeds. And you must let go, be patient with yourself and nurture the seeds that you plant. By the way, if you do not take personal responsibility for planting your own seeds, something will still grow. Weeds. Or potentially worse, something you allowed someone else to plant!

Step Three: Applying the Knowledge of Your Beliefs

Your last challenge is to apply the knowledge of your belief systems to the way you do things every day. You have raised your level of awareness of what your personal beliefs are and where they are taking you. You've taken an inventory of your beliefs, discovering where your beliefs came from and letting your emotions tell you which beliefs you need to embrace and

The Contented Achiever

which ones you need to challenge. Now it's time to make a commitment to change the beliefs that are holding you back. Let them go. Refuse to cling to them for another moment.

Of course, the universe abhors a void, so whenever you eliminate something from your life, you must replace it with something else. Someone trying, for instance, to give up smoking, might replace smoking with over-eating. (Not a good idea to replace one unhealthy habit for another. That's why this takes some planning!) Another option might be to replace smoking with exercise, or doing volunteer work, or another activity that would be constructive and make you feel good.

The same is true of changing beliefs. For example, a friend of mine enjoyed variety in her work, and she happily took on many interesting projects. Her belief, however, was that she would never

> **NEVER UNDERESTIMATE THE POWER OF SELF-TALK.**

have enough time to do everything she wanted. She constantly worried that there wouldn't be enough time. In reality, every project she undertook got done. So, rather than continue to make herself miserable by thinking about how she wouldn't have enough time, she began telling herself, "I have plenty of time to do everything I want." Anytime she heard herself saying, "Oh, no, how will I ever do all this?" she would immediately say out loud, "I have plenty of time to do everything I want." She found if she got focused and took one step at a time, she could achieve enormous quantities of work. Never underestimate the power of positive self-talk.

Plant new seeds by reading good books, listening to good tapes, trying new experiences and meeting uplifting people. Make a list right now and set aside some high quality time to examine your beliefs, understand your beliefs and change the beliefs that are not getting you where you want to go in life. Make today and everyday an extraordinary day in your life. Reflect . . . consider . . . decide . . . and act!

How to Change Other People

Now that you understand belief systems, you may feel moved to use this wonderful new knowledge to fix the other people in your life. You may say, "Well, I've fixed myself, now I can fix all those other people who are keeping me from achieving my goals."

THE QUICKEST AND BEST WAY TO CHANGE SOMEONE ELSE IS TO CHANGE SOMETHING ABOUT YOURSELF.

The beauty of this program is that if you do it thoroughly, you will be very busy addressing your own issues, and you will have no time for looking at anyone else. Because not only is fixing others impossible, luckily, it's also unnecessary. Be who you are, and be willing to let others be who they are. If you are

The Contented Achiever

convinced that you need to change other people, work on yourself. The quickest and best way to change someone else is to change something about yourself.

If you are convinced that another person is wrong, there is always the chance it could just be a case of mistaken certainty. Or, perhaps, the two of you just have significantly different belief systems. The Native Americans said, "To truly understand another, you must walk in his moccasins." We've all witnessed what we consider an inappropriate action on the part of someone else and asked ourselves -- Why did they do that? What is wrong with them? One possible answer is that they thought that their action was totally appropriate. You may be the one who does not understand.

Recently I heard a story about the value of determining the appropriateness of people's actions before making a decision about the "rightness" or "wrongness" of their actions. If you saw a house on fire, and a group of people with axes were tearing the house apart and flooding it with water, you would probably quickly decide that their actions were totally appropriate. But what if a group of angry people were doing the same thing, and the house was not on fire? You would probably label it vandalism. The first group of people believed in their mission and their actions were driven by their love of their community and sense of duty. The second group of people believed in their mission and their actions were driven by hatred. It was not difficult to see the beliefs of both groups.

The Contented Achiever

If someone is doing something that can be categorized as bad or evil, you still will not change them without understanding the root cause of their behavior -- their belief system.

Strangely, it always seems to be easiest to see the beliefs of others. How simple it is to spend your time watching everyone else, judging what they are doing, and deciding how they should change! Interestingly, if you spend your time working on yourself, the people in your life will magically mirror your goals.

Bifocals Work Best

Corrective lenses can help you see not only up close, but also far away, so that you can anticipate how your current beliefs will affect your life in the long run. With this clearer view, you can align your beliefs and your goals, and make them become visible in your life. You have the power to create your own electricity, and to light up your own life.

The Contented Achiever

POINTS TO PONDER

* What lessons will people learn by "observing what you do?"

* What beliefs are taking you in the right direction in life? The wrong direction?

* What are you clinging to that you need to let go of?

* How much time and energy do you consume trying to "fix" other people?

* What new beliefs do you need to embrace to make your vision a reality?

> "THE MORE TRANQUIL WE BECOME,
> THE GREATER IS OUR SUCCESS,
> OUR INFLUENCE, OUR POWER FOR GOOD."
>
> JAMES ALLEN

Chapter Five
Clutter, Immobilizers and Other Useless Things

Overcoming the Overwhelming

Did you know that there is a culprit that sneaks into your life and steals your productivity and peace of mind? It is a common, ordinary, everyday issue, but it takes on immense importance when you understand how it saps your energy and drains you of your ability to create the life you desire. You may be so accustomed to it that you don't recognize its cumulative devastating effect. It's like a cancer that has not yet been diagnosed. The thing is called clutter!

Clutterberg, Dead Ahead on the Starboard Side!

There are two kinds of clutter that ambush people. They are:

The Contented Achiever

- Physical clutter, and

- Mental immobilizers

If you've spent any time in the South you may be familiar with kudzu. Kudzu is a beautiful and insidious green vine that will completely obscure houses, vehicles, trees and even living beings who stand still too long. Physical clutter is the "kudzu" of the office and the home environment. It loves drawers, closets, attics, basements, and garages. It feels right at home anywhere else in the house. It likes the trunk of the car, the glove box, back seat and under the seat. It is a ubiquitous culprit. Physical clutter is just the tip of the iceberg. Beneath the surface of visible chaos you may find a huge chunk of mental clutter waiting to tear a gaping hole in your dreams. Whether it's clutter you can see, or the kind you can't, it provides the fuel for confusion, disorder and turmoil in both your external and internal world. Left unchecked, it can eventually turn into a titanic problem. And it won't go away or melt on its own. You must take action to get rid of it.

Use It, Love It, or Let It Go

Physical clutter is probably lurking about you this very moment doing what it does best . . . serving no useful purpose and creating unnecessary stress.

The Contented Achiever

It can be stacked, stuffed, stashed and spread all over your office and home. It attacks rich people, poor people, males, females, bosses and workers with equal vengeance. At one time or another, it steals the very life energy needed to function effectively from almost everyone.

Clutter ties you to the past, keeps you from enjoying the present and threatens to rob your future.

Webster's dictionary defines the verb "clutter" as:

"To fill or cover with scattered or disordered things that impede movement or reduce effectiveness."

The noun "clutter" doesn't fare much better. The same dictionary defines it as:

"A crowded or confused mass or collection of things."

Clutter falls into many categories:

- Things you don't need, use or love having around.

- Things untidy or disorganized.

- Too many things in too small a space.

- Things that are lying around dormant and unfinished or overdue.

- Things that cause confusion, frustration and chaos.

- Things that you should have tossed but have somehow justified keeping.

- Things that immobilize you.

No matter how you look at clutter, it won't win any popularity contests. Like a boa constrictor that slowly wraps around its victim, it squeezes the productivity and energy out of individuals, small businesses and large corporations.

A Few Neat Solutions

For some years I have trained people one-on-one to remove clutter from their offices. In just three or four hours they can create a working environment that is not only set up for maximum efficiency, effectiveness and work-life enjoyment, but also reduces stress dramatically.

In learning how to help clients with this problem, I conducted extensive research on the resources available to solve the clutter problem. Here are a few of the tips that seem to be common to most of the books, tapes and courses studied:

- Get started! Cut the problem up into small pieces. The idea of tackling your entire office can be overwhelming and result in project indigestion. Cleaning up one drawer a day or cleaning off your desktop is digestible.

The Contented Achiever

- Pick a place to organize and stick with it until you are finished. If you're cleaning out a closet and find something that belongs in another room, don't take it to the other room until you finish dealing with the closet. Put several containers around you to temporarily store similar items. One container might be for all things that belong somewhere else. One would be for discarded items. When you finish the closet, then take the container to the other rooms and drop off the items. Stay focused on one area and finish it.

- Ruthlessly throw things away. If you haven't used or worn something in a year, or at most two, you can probably live without it. Learn that you can enjoy letting go of things as much as you enjoy acquiring them. Find a stack of old magazines that have been nagging you to read them for months. You know, it's that stack that you are going to get around to "one of these days." The stack that makes you feel guilty every single time you see it. Drop the entire stack in the trash or recycling container and celebrate the fact that your life will go on just fine without reading them. You can also rejoice in the fact that you have learned a new skill . . . discarding!

- Give things away. Help someone in need and you can usually get a tax deduction, too. For example, give away the 80% of your clothes that you never wear and probably never will.

- If possible, get rid of anything that reminds you of unpleasant memories. Why keep old photos of people or events that generate negative emotions for you?

- Finish anything unfinished or discard it: the half-built trellis, the needlepoint you started when your children were small, the brochures from the cruise that you never took in 1986.

- Create a simple filing system that allows you to find things when you need them.

GETTING RID OF CLUTTER IS NOT ROCKET SCIENCE. THE HARD PART IS GETTING STARTED.

I could go on and on, but I think you get the point. Getting rid of clutter is not rocket science. The hard part is usually getting started. To encourage you to get started, let's consider some of the benefits of eliminating clutter from your life.

EXTERNAL BENEFITS	INTERNAL BENEFITS
• You can find your car keys.	• Reduced anxiety.
• You may not have to buy that bigger house after all.	• Increased feeling of peace, tranquility and serenity.
• You will save money. You won't have to go out and buy things that you know you already have "somewhere."	• Increased productivity.
	• Increased ability to concentrate.
• You may be able to reduce your taxes.	• Increased energy.
• You can give up your storage bin.	• Greater fulfillment in higher quality work.
• You can easily handle the unexpected guests who call and say they are "just dropping by" without the frantic clean up that usually occurs between the time they call and the time they arrive.	• You can use the time you formerly spent looking for things to pursue your passion in life.

As I mentioned, there are many resources that can help you learn how to minimize or eliminate this problem from your life. Take action now! Find one of these resources and tackle this issue today. If you do not have the time to start your de-cluttering project today, at least take the time now to schedule the time to do it soon. Develop a positive attitude about this undertaking. It is simple to do, it is a practical thing to do and the benefits are substantial.

Telling Yourself "Clutter Lies?"

Many people do not understand that clutter in their life is like an invisible ball and chain. I am convinced that most people do not even know this is a big problem in their life because they cannot see it. How many of these "clutter lies" have you been telling yourself?

- If I file it I will forget where I put it.

- Each stack is a project, and the more projects I have the more successful I will be.

- A clean desk is the sign of a sick mind.

- Out of sight, out of mind.

- A messy office makes me look busy and important.

- As soon as I find what I am looking for and get some spare time I will organize this mess.

- I have been operating this way for years and it doesn't really bother me.

The Clutter Removal Epiphany

When I first started conducting training sessions to help people organize their offices, I was primarily focused on eliminating physical clutter; however, my work in this area quickly led to some interesting discoveries. After one session with a client, I asked my traditional wrap up question: "How do you feel right now?" The client looked at me calmly and seriously and replied, "You have lifted a burden from my soul." I looked around to see if Reverend Billy Graham had walked into the room . . . he had not. Being a person with an intense interest in spiritual matters, I thought that her response was very interesting. Here I was, teaching her simple techniques about how to handle paperwork and eliminate clutter from her office space and she was having what appeared to be a quasi-spiritual experience. My internal curiosity alarm went off. I stored her comment in my memory bank. We chatted a few more minutes, finished the training session and I left.

The Pattern of Peacefulness

That night I kept thinking about her comment and it made me think of other comments that clients had made. Some typical responses were:

The Contented Achiever

"I feel a sense of tranquility."

"I feel peaceful."

"I feel a sense of serenity."

"I feel organized for the first time in years."

"I feel focused and in control of my life."

"I feel great."

"I feel energetic."

It didn't take much of a mental leap to recognize a pattern. Facts are always nice to know but patterns usually end up being the best teachers in life. What was going on? Why did training people to be organized and get rid of physical clutter result in responses of this nature?

The Rest of the Story . . .
Other By-Products of a Lifted Burden

Within a week, the woman who experienced the "lifted burden" called me and told me some other interesting things. After the session she went home, and her husband said she looked different and seemed happier and more relaxed than he had seen her in quite a while. Over the next week people came into her office and told her she looked great and asked her if she was working out, taking vitamins or doing something different to improve her health.

My curiosity was building. I asked others that I had trained about their "after effects," and got similar responses. Here I

The Contented Achiever

was just trying to help them get rid of clutter and some of them were talking about how it was changing their lives.

One "graduate" was getting a lot of grief from his co-workers about his clean desk and office. They were saying things like, "You must not have enough to do," and, "Are you leaving the firm?" When I tried to console him and tell him not to worry about his co-worker's comments, he looked directly at me and calmly, peacefully, with an intense tone of commitment said, "I haven't had this much control over my life in the thirty years that I have been working. I don't care what they say. My new habits are here to stay."

> **CLUTTER CHOKES PEOPLE'S PRODUCTIVITY AND GENERATES SO MUCH STRESS THAT IT CAN EVEN CAUSE PHYSICAL AND PSYCHOLOGICAL PROBLEMS.**

Clutter is a much bigger problem than most people realize. The iceberg is huge and runs deep under the surface. It chokes people's productivity and generates so much stress that it can even cause physical and psychological problems.

Dig Up the Roots

The more I thought about the effects of clutter on people's lives, the more I realized that it was the root cause of many

other problems that negatively impact personal productivity, job satisfaction and happiness with life in general.

Once again we have uncovered a simple solution to a big problem. Most people just don't get around to dealing with the clutter in their lives. They don't take the time to deal with it because they are not aware of how much it is affecting their lives. It is as if they are looking through a lens that makes the problem invisible. Look around; think about it and I think that you will find that clutter is the root cause of many of your problems. I have now talked to people who have tried some very complex and expensive techniques to solve problems that the removal of clutter solved almost immediately. Buying a complex solution, by itself, will only un-clutter your bank account. Never discount the power of a simple idea.

Don't look for another solution when one is right under your nose. I have personally had too many people tell me that they never knew how much clutter was bothering them until I helped them remove it from their office. I can see the result of cleaning up clutter in people's faces. I can hear it in their voices. I have learned to predict which ones will call me two weeks later and tell me stories about how they finished their offices, and then went home and started cleaning up the clutter in their house. Removing clutter will pull many problems up by the roots. They will often disappear on their own.

The Contented Achiever

Mental Immobilizers and Other Useless Things

We have already made reference to another one of the great immobilizers in life -- GETTING STARTED.

Here is a cosmic rule of the universe for you:

IF YOU NEVER START SOMETHING, YOU WILL NEVER FINISH IT!

Develop the ability to apply the
LAW OF THE "DOs":

DO!
DO IT!
DO IT RIGHT!
DO IT RIGHT NOW!
YOU DO IT RIGHT NOW!

Generate that burst of energy needed to launch the next event in the chain of events that will get you from where you are to where you want to go. Remember what we said about how it can take more fuel to get an airplane off the ground than it does to get to the final destination? You can see this pattern everywhere in your life. It applies to starting a project, starting a book, starting a diet, and starting anything that you desire to accomplish. The key is to start!

Think of the energy it takes to get the space shuttle off the ground and into orbit. Normally when you see the shuttle being launched in movies or in documentary films, the music illustrates the kind of emotions that you experience when you are launching your dreams. The background music always seems to be intense during the lift-off and remains intense until the shuttle achieves orbit. Then it becomes calm, serene, relaxing and peaceful. When launching your dreams, these feelings are your inner guides telling you that you are in orbit and on the right course.

Lighting the Candle

To launch a rocket, you must "light the candle" and get started. John F. Kennedy lit a candle when he proclaimed in his inaugural speech that we would put a man on the moon by the end of the decade. His words set in motion one of the most ambitious projects that mankind ever attempted. Now, part of you might be saying, "I'm no Jack Kennedy. After all, Kennedy was the President of the United States. He could go around doing things like that and it worked for him. What good will it do me to light candles without the resources to back up my desires?" There is a story about a more down to earth example of this principle at work.

The Contented Achiever

Overfed, Overwhelmed and Undermotivated

It was Thanksgiving Day. The family was together. We had cooked all day. We were now at that moment when the meal was finished and most of us were silently asking, "Why did I eat that last helping?" We were stuffed, on the edge of overeating misery. Every pot, pan, glass, utensil and dish in the house was dirty. Every surface in the kitchen and dining room was covered with the remnants of our feast. We were all in the lethargy zone, belts loosened, eyelids heavy, "tar-pit humans" stuck in our chairs.

The mess wasn't going to clean up itself, but we just couldn't get started. With the last ounce of energy I had, I got up and lit a candle. I don't mean this figuratively. I actually got up, got a candle from the living room, struck a match and lit it. I said, "Well, someone had to light a fire and get this group going." The rest of the group laughed, and the mood began to change ever so slightly. I got up and put on some upbeat music. Other people began to move. We all started laughing about the situation and someone said, "Let's do it!" We attacked the mess with the fury of a thousand jungle beasts. (Maybe we weren't that energetic, but I always wanted to work that line into a story somehow.) Before we knew it the mission was completed.

To this day, we all joke about the lighting of the candle. We probably couldn't tell you what we ate or other details of that

Thanksgiving Day, but although years have passed, none of us have forgotten the highlight of that particular Thanksgiving -- the fun of cleaning up.

Fighting off immobilization isn't a matter of coming up with some grand scheme to solve world hunger, or being John Kennedy, or launching a rocket to the moon. All you've got to do is light that candle inside you and take the next best step. One small step often generates the energy that you need to take the next one, and so on, and so on. It's a matter of becoming skilled at getting started. Take positive actions, don't just have positive thoughts.

> ONE SMALL STEP OFTEN GENERATES THE ENERGY THAT YOU NEED TO TAKE THE NEXT ONE.

What Keeps People From Starting?

There appears to be an almost endless number of reasons or excuses for why people have trouble getting started. Below is a list of some of the more prominent ones that we will address in the remainder of this chapter:

- Staircase thinking

- Too much past/future thinking

The Contented Achiever

- Fearful thinking

- Perfectionism

Staircase Thinking

This is simply another version of the Chinese proverb "A journey of a thousand miles must begin with a single step." It's simple: If you are on the first floor of your home and you desire to be on the second floor, you may go up the staircase one step at a time. If you're a "Type A" personality, you may take several steps at once. But even if you're hyper, you probably will not try to leap the entire staircase in a single bound. So why do we try to do projects by jumping directly from the first floor to the second floor?

I admire visionaries. I think the world needs them. However, I admire, respect and want to learn from those people who are what I call balanced visionaries. Frustrated visionaries stand at the bottom of the stairs doing nothing because they can't just leap to the top and land in the middle of their vision. Their frustration immobilizes them so that they can't even begin the journey. How sad. And how unnecessary!

Balanced visionaries see the grand vision of the future, and then use passion and drive to come back to the present and focus on the best next step that must be taken to "light the candle." Stair-CASE thinking will not get the job done. It takes stair-STEP thinking to convert a vision into reality. The balanced visionary enjoys each step along the way, in the present moment, knowing that the journey is what it is all about, and that the reward of closure is forthcoming.

Too Much "Past/Future" Thinking

It's true: Those who fail to study history may be doomed to repeat it. And yes, you need to blueprint your future by thinking about it.

As management guru Peter Drucker said, "The best way to predict the future is to create it." The only time you can physically create anything is in the present. Therefore, you must spend the majority of your time in the present moment. Past/future thinking keeps you from getting started in two ways:

- Regrets keep you in the past.

- Desires keep you in the future.

You cannot be two places at once; therefore, if you spend too much time focusing on regrets and desires, you cannot be in the present where the first step is always taken and progress is always attained.

The Contented Achiever

If you spend a lot of time regretting the projects that you started in the past that are still unfinished, you will be hesitant to start something new. Let them go! Do not allow events that occurred in the past to drain your energy in the present. Desires are the "if only's" that keep you from starting. Have you ever said,

- If only I had some money, I could invest in this new venture.

- If only I had finished college, I could get a better job.

- If only I had more time, I could . . .

If only's represent past regrets or future wishes. Learn from the past, have fun thinking about the future, but rely on present thinking and present action to get the job done. Get focused, be resilient, and never give up.

Fearful Thinking

Fear paralyzes. It renders people immobile, inoperable and powerless.

If you are a human being, you understand what fear can do to a person, because fear is always present in your life to some degree. But there are two kinds of fear:

- Useful or healthy fear (constructive)

- Useless or unhealthy fear (destructive)

Like stress, a healthy level of fear is necessary. It keeps most of us from doing stupid things like jumping off cliffs or picking up rattlesnakes. The absence of some level of healthy fear can be detrimental.

Here's a little something interesting about snakes. Snakes don't want to encounter humans any more than humans want to encounter snakes. An emergency room doctor said that women are rarely bitten, but occasionally, they accidentally startle a rattlesnake and the result is a bite on the ankle or lower leg. Men, however, are often treated for bites on the face, neck, arms and hands. The doctor explained, "Whoever is the drunkest usually gets bitten. They usually get bitten because they are playing with the snake." Alcohol can artificially remove healthy fears and that can be detrimental.

A reasonable level of fear can protect you from the snake bites of the world. And fears can not only benefit you in this way; working through them also builds inner strength and is accompanied by significant rewards.

But unhealthy fear stops us dead in our tracks, just as effectively as seeing a rattlesnake.

The Contented Achiever

Unhealthy fears are those that keep us from growing, changing or simply taking a step toward action. I have heard people
talk about their fear of:

-What will other people think?
-What will happen if it doesn't work?
-What will happen if it does work, and then I have to
   keep up the facade?
-What if people realize that I'm not as smart as they
   thought?
-What if I can't really do it?

Worrying about "what if" is living in the future. If you take
the first step, any number of
other things will result, and you
cannot anticipate them all.
"What if" is as useless as its
previously discussed cousin, "if

THE ANTIDOTE
TO FEAR
IS KNOWLEDGE.

only." Do not waste your valuable time on these useless mental immobilizers.

Strangely, when we ask ourselves "what if," we usually focus
on something negative happening. Why don't we project good
things happening? I have heard that of the bad things we worry
about, only 5 percent ever actually occur.

People do not fear what they understand. To carry on with the
reptile theme, if you don't believe this, watch the TV program

The Contented Achiever

called *Crocodile Hunter.* The star of this show obviously understands snakes, and because of his knowledge of the creatures he remains cool, calm and confident as he reaches inside a dark hole full of poisonous critters. His knowledge of these creatures has allowed him to effectively deal with fear. The same principle can help you build inner strength and lead you to great rewards.

If fear is holding you back from getting started on something, try to raise your level of awareness of the fear and pinpoint exactly what your fear is all about. Remember that fear is usually just a by-product of negative beliefs (I'm not good enough), so try to challenge your belief and it will help you challenge your fear. This will help you pinpoint what you need to learn next to deal with this immobilizer.

> **"WHAT WOULD YOU ATTEMPT TO DO IF YOU**
> **KNEW YOU WOULD NOT FAIL?"**
> DR. ROBERT SCHULLER

Perfectionism

Trying to be a perfectionist can slow you down or stop you dead in your tracks. The pursuit of ongoing improvement and excellence is a healthy activity. The pursuit of perfection is a neurotic activity.

I learned a term in high school mathematics that illustrates a great way to approach projects and success in general. An asymptotic line on a graph keeps getting closer and closer to the axis of the graph—but it never touches the axis. It's like always dividing the distance between two points in half. You will get closer and closer but there will always be half of something left. Strive to asymptotically approach success, and eliminate any sense of frustration that you cannot be at a point called perfection.

Are You Gaining Energy or Draining Energy?

Can we cover everything that immobilizes people in one chapter? Of course not; however, the immobilizers that we have discussed in this chapter all have one thing in common -- they drain your energy. We all have different immobilizers which should be carefully identified. Become sensitive to and aware of what drains your energy. Once you are aware of the things that drain your energy, you can seek the knowledge to understand them and take actions to deal with the problem. Remember that the job of a problem is to get your attention. Pay attention to what clutter, immobilizers and

> THE JOB OF A PROBLEM IS TO GET YOUR ATTENTION. FIND OUT WHAT CLUTTER, IMMOBILIZERS AND OTHER USELESS THINGS ARE TRYING TO TELL YOU.

other useless things are trying to tell you.

Don't keep clutter stashed in your drawers or stuffed in your brain. It starts out as a small problem and if left untreated, it spreads through your entire life and robs you of precious resources.

The Contented Achiever

POINTS TO PONDER

✖ How would you feel if your working space and living space were totally clutter free?

✖ What would be required for you to remove the physical clutter from your life? What would be the benefits of removing the clutter?

✖ What is keeping you from starting projects that are important to your success? Can you erase these barriers?

✖ What immobilizing fears do you have and why?

✖ Reject "if only" and "what if" immobilizers - - they are counterproductive to accomplishment.

✖ Get started!

"YOU MUST HAVE A ROOM, OR A CERTAIN HOUR
OR SO A DAY, WHERE YOU DON'T KNOW WHAT
WAS IN THE NEWSPAPERS THAT MORNING . . .
A PLACE WHERE YOU CAN SIMPLY EXPERIENCE
AND BRING FORTH WHAT YOU ARE AND
WHAT YOU MIGHT BE."

JOSEPH CAMPBELL

The Contented Achiever

Chapter Six
Creating an Environment for Success

Kids Do the Darnedest Things

It was the best of toys; it was the worst of toys. It was also one of the most unsightly things that ever found a place in my children's hearts and in the living room of our home. They called it "Big-Box."

Our old washing machine broke down, and when they delivered the new one to our house I had the brilliant idea to keep the box . . . for a few days. I thought it would be fun for the children to play with . . . for a few days. We cut holes for doors and windows, turned it upside down and decided to put it in the living room . . . for a few days.

In just a few days I realized that I had totally underestimated the drawing power of an upside down washing machine box to the fertile minds of two young children. As an authority figure for the family, I put my foot down. It had to go, it was history, and it was out of here! Little did I realize how many tears four small eyes could produce. Those of you who are parents probably already know the rest of this story. Big-Box wasn't going anywhere . . . for over a year!

Big-Box, the Sequel

When my son went off to college and got his own apartment, he said, "Dad, I need a washer and dryer." We gave him our old ones and bought new ones. Well, those who fail to study history are doomed to repeat it; those who fail to remember history are also doomed to repeat it. Sure enough, I put both boxes in the living room for my third child, a five-year old. Oh, well, it was just . . . for a few days.

Out-of-the-Box Thinkers, Thinking in the Box

When I make a mistake, I try to remember to ask myself, "What should I be learning from this?" When I looked at "Big-Boxville," I started asking that and other questions. I wondered what made these boxes so appealing to children? I started observing my daughter when she played with the boxes to see what I could learn.

The Contented Achiever

Several years ago one branch of the military service advertised that "It's not just a job, it's an adventure!" Big-Box was not just a box to my daughter, it was an adventure. One day she was a storeowner. She owned a store called Box-Mart. She would poke her head through the window and make a sale to a passing parent who paid with imaginary money. Another day she was a schoolteacher surrounded with stuffed animal students. Another day she was a doctor, a waitress, a chef and a mom. This was her place and her space.

Although Mom and Dad called a place in the house "her room," and filled it with expensive toys, she never quite had that feeling of comfort, control and joy that she experienced when she was in the "Big-Box." At five years old, she knew exactly how to create an environment for success and happiness.

Professionally, I spend a lot of my time helping people think out-of-the-box; my own children seem to do their best creative thinking in-the-box.

It didn't take long for me to drift back to my youth and think of all the times I had sat in a box, or under the blankets thrown over a couple of chairs, or in the tree house at my grandparents' farm. Suddenly I understood completely. It wasn't the box or the blanket or the tree house that was important, it was the personal space, the environment, the feeling you had when you were in your space. Why does growing up make us forget so many good ideas?

The Contented Achiever

"Method Writing"

Why does growing up make us forget so many good ideas? When I asked myself that, the thought "method acting" flashed through my mind. For those of you who don't remember exactly what method acting is (I didn't), I looked it up in the dictionary. It is a system of acting in which the actor recalls emotions and reactions from his past experiences and utilizes them in the role he is playing. Then I thought, if you can method act, why can't you method write? The trick would be to just access those feelings I had in my childhood. But . . . my guess is, it has probably been at least forty years since I have sat inside an upside down washing machine box.

During the Christmas holidays, my daughter got distracted from the washer and dryer boxes, which gave me an opportunity to stash Big-Box in the attic. But then something weird happened. I started wondering about the power of that piece of cardboard. As you might imagine, curiosity not only can kill a cat, it can get a "perfectly normal" leading edge baby boomer to drag the box out of the attic and sit in it.

When my wife discovered that I had spent some time "in the box," she began questioning my definition of the words "perfectly normal." Disparaging thoughts aside, guess what: I discovered that after all of these years, the box still works!

Throughout this book are simple, inexpensive ideas to create

The Contented Achiever

peace of mind. If you don't count the price of a washing machine, I may have discovered another one.

Out-of-the-Box Writing

Although I tell you this story half-kidding, I was actually fascinated by what went on in my mind when I sat in the box. It took me back to some childhood memories that I had not thought of in years. It allowed me to create the same feeling that you get when you are meditating. It was actually more fun than I thought it would be. It is a great place to minimize distractions and relax. All sorts of interesting possibilities revealed themselves inside the box. And that is the point of this chapter. Everybody needs an environment where they can go to discover their possibilities. Whether thinking in-the-box or out-of-the-box, make the quest for discovery a priority.

What in the World Can I Do about My Environment?

I have always admired people who want to change the world, but it sounds like a pretty big task to me. I want the ozone problem fixed as much as the next guy; however, fixing it just didn't turn out to be my purpose in life. It is someone's purpose, and I'm happy about that. But my purpose is to learn, teach and share. Those are the "little things" that make up my life. I'm not a doctor, lawyer, fireman, policeman, or ozonefixerman. I am a teacher. I teach through books, speeches, seminars and most importantly, through my actions. That is my current choice of "what I want to be when I grow up." Although I reserve the right to change this fluid commitment anytime I feel like it, right now I have to take personal responsibility for creating an environment where these things can and will be nurtured. That's the field I have to plow, those are the seeds that I must sow and nurture.

I made this choice by following those inner guides we talked about earlier, my positive and negative emotions. I made this choice because I feel good when I do it.

Like most of us, my first few "what I want to be when I grow up choices" were made by others. I know that ultimately I decided to major in a certain field in college, or take a certain job, or take another job for more money; however, I didn't pay enough attention to my internal guides when I made these decisions. I paid a lot of attention to external guides. Like most people, I made many decisions based on what somebody else thought was a good idea for me. I let other people design my environment for success.

At those points in my life, I didn't understand much about making good career decisions, but I did understand how to nurture the choices that I'd made. Financially, things seemed to be working out pretty good for me. However, pretty good is not good enough! It would always be just a matter of time

The Contented Achiever

before the guides would be telling me to move on from "pretty goodness" and go for mastery!

There's a Place for Us

To make choices that feel right for you, you must start by creating an environment where you can let your imagination and feelings guide you to the next level in life - - - whether a Big-Box or a Maui beach. THERE IS ALWAYS A NEXT LEVEL IN LIFE NO MATTER HOW SUCCESSFUL YOU ARE. It should be a priority to craft your own next level! Make sure it is a higher, nobler level and that you passionately want to go.

Your Big-Box might be a reading area set aside in one room of your house. Perhaps it's an office or meditation area where you can be alone. It could be a special park where you can sit and think, walk, or write in a journal. It might be a church, or a library. What's important is that you find that place that works for you and spend time there on a regular basis, letting your mind expand.

> IT'S IMPORTANT TO FIND A PLACE THAT WORKS FOR YOU AND SPEND TIME THERE ON A REGULAR BASIS.

Change the World?

If you want to have any chance of changing the world, you are going to have to change your world first. You must take personal responsibility for your environment. You may not be the center of the universe, but you are the center of your universe. You may think this sounds selfish and self-centered, but I don't mean be the center of your universe in a childish and arrogant way. I mean it in the same sense that flight attendants do when they tell you that "in the event of an emergency, put your oxygen mask on first and then place one on your child." You can't help your children if you pass out first.

> **YOU MAY NOT BE THE CENTER OF THE UNIVERSE, BUT YOU ARE THE CENTER OF YOUR UNIVERSE.**

I often think of this concept as the Law of Gifts. In dealing with tangibles, people usually understand that you can't give away something that you do not have. However, they often forget this rule when they are dealing with intangibles. For example, they actually think they can give away happiness, love, joy, knowledge and other intangibles when they do not have it themselves. Not possible. Even if it appears that you are successfully doing this, any positive effects of such a gift are illusions and will not last. So let's focus on creating the right environment for you before we try to solve world hunger.

The Contented Achiever

If you want to nurture your spiritual goals, financial goals, intellectual goals or any other goals, you must create an environment where they can survive and prosper.

Environmental Concentric Circles

When you have found your special place, you can begin to explore possibilities and to think of the various areas of your life and how you feel about each one. What will it take to create a physical and mental environment that is most supportive to your goals?

One way to begin creating your environment for success is to think of your environment as a series of concentric circles. Start at the center of the circle and work your way to the outer parts of the circle.

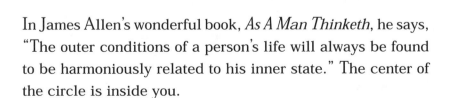

In James Allen's wonderful book, *As A Man Thinketh*, he says, "The outer conditions of a person's life will always be found to be harmoniously related to his inner state." The center of the circle is inside you.

People use different techniques to work on their inner state. They may get involved in meditation, therapy, hobbies, reading and various other activities. If what you do is working for you, by all means keep on doing it. Some techniques are quite expensive and some cost little or nothing. Let's pursue a technique that I believe is quite affordable and effective.

High Impact Center Circle Activity

In an earlier chapter, we briefly discussed a technique called morning pages from a book by Julia Cameron called *The Artist's Way*. I don't know why it works; I don't know how it works, but I know it works. The simple technique she outlines in her book suggests that you hand write three pages every morning with no concern for grammar, punctuation, logic or anything else. Just keep your hand moving and you will find that the most amazing things emerge from your center. The book is full of other great exercises and ideas and I recommend it highly; however, morning pages are absolutely amazing. It is a life changing technique that will help you create an internal environment for success. (And Ms. Cameron's book is cheaper than a new washer and dryer that you would have to buy to get the boxes!)

Traveling Outward

As you are ready to move to the next circle, you get to choose

The Contented Achiever

what the next most important one is for you. As a matter of fact, it is critically important that you choose it. But let's discuss what might be a few more of the outer rings in your life.

In my case, the next ring is physical, because when I feel clean and healthy, and within my acceptable weight range, I feel good. I am not saying this is for everyone; however, I am one of those people who even shave on Saturday. On the other hand, I have a friend who actually likes to look slightly unshaven. He goes to a barbershop every Saturday to have his week's growth of facial hair carefully groomed to a slightly unshaven look. The point is, keep your body in the condition that makes you feel good. That may include shaving or not shaving, make-up or no make-up, exercise, diet or whatever works for you. If you don't take care of your physical body, where are you going to live?!

A Space Full of Compromises

The next ring might be your home, car or your office. People who travel regularly on business or for pleasure can also create this space on the road. For example, an investment of a few hundred dollars per year in airline terminal clubs is an indulgence that has made airports less stressful and a more positive space for work and rest. I also take along items like photos and small mementos that make the hotel room a more welcoming and positive place. Learn to create portable space both mentally and materially.

> **GIVE YOURSELF THE GIFT OF A CHAOS-FREE PLACE IN WHICH TO GROW.**

We have already discussed the value of keeping your space clutter free, defining what shouldn't be in your space. Give yourself the gift of a chaos-free place in which to grow. But you must also focus on what should be in your space. Ideally your environment should include no compromises.

Right after her college graduation, my wife had lunch with her mother and one of her mother's friends. (When you graduate from college, people are quick to give you advice about life and things in general.) As my wife discussed a purchase she was considering, she told her lunch companions about her dilemma.

She was shopping for a table. "I've found one I really like, but it's very expensive and much more than I should spend. However, there's a similar one at another store. It doesn't have quite the same look, but it's quite a bit cheaper." Her mother's friend gave her some sound advice. "I used to think that way and I woke up at forty and realized that I lived in a house full of compromises. Wait until you can afford the one you truly love."

How many things are in your home, office, garage, drawers or

The Contented Achiever

closets that you just don't like? How many of these things represent compromises in your life? You knew better when you acquired them. They were on sale or less expensive than what you really wanted. To create an environment for success, you must begin minimizing and eventually eliminating compromises. Compromises are the worst sort of clutter. They not only represent physical claims on your energy, but they also represent mental claims on your energy. Begin removing compromises from your life and fill your environment with things you love. Of course, this applies to intangibles as well.

What's the Hurry

Some think that the rapid acquiring of material possessions is the way to go, even if they must make compromises along the way. So many people seem unwilling or unable to delay gratification. I vote to delay. Any inconvenience or postponement of pleasure is a small price to pay for the ultimate joy felt in owning a high quality version of the item a bit later. This delay may also represent a prudent opportunity to pay cash for the nicer item rather than co-owning with a bank!

Defining Your Circles

I believe that an author, a leader, an advisor or a friend is headed in the wrong direction when they promise you a certain path to success. People are unique; therefore, paths to success must be unique. Nobody can or should try to design your unique path. Others can serve as a "lighthouse" for you, shining their light and showing you a path to success, but you must choose to take the path that makes the most sense for you.

> **AS A SUCCESSFUL PERSON MATURES, THEY TAKE MORE AND MORE RESPONSIBILITY FOR THE CREATION OF THEIR ENVIRONMENT.**

In each of your circles, create the situations that most support your goals. Your next concentric circle may be your spiritual environment, intellectual environment, financial environment or any other area of your life. Everyone needs a place where they can go, use their imagination and discover their possibilities. Everyone must be accountable for creating their own personal environment for success. As a successful person matures, they take more and more responsibility for the creation of their environment.

People Need People

It's inevitable: In many of your life circles, you will bump into other people. Some will support your goals; some will not. No matter, they will all contribute immeasurably to your being able to accomplish your goals in one way or another.

The Contented Achiever

My high school anthropology teacher told me I had the talent and potential to succeed in college, but I would have to work harder and apply myself (that was three degrees ago). Conversely, a graduate management professor told me I would never write anything worth reading (that was before I authored many books and articles). Build on and cherish the positive influences and use the comments of negative influences as "jet fuel" to prove them wrong.

Healthy Materialism

I want to make a confession to you. I am a philosophical thinker who likes material things. I have not run across a rule that says you must be poor to be successful. I believe you can be poor in a material sense and be successful; however, I do not consider it a requirement. I personally choose abundance, consistent with our contented achiever concept.

The principles outlined in this book have always provided me with beautiful homes, nice cars, nice clothes and other things that money can buy. The great thing about creating material wealth is that you have the opportunity to understand that these things can bring you joy, but taken alone, they cannot sustain joy and inner peace. But I want to go on record as encouraging you to go for as much wealth as you can if that is what you want. This book is to help you get what you want, so if money is your thing, go for it and do not apologize for it. On the other hand, if you are not materialistic at all, I recommend you consider going for abundance anyway and then give your wealth away. Just don't forget all of the other aspects of your environment that must be nurtured in order for you to enjoy a life of material wealth.

Tending Your Success Garden

Your environment is your life's garden. It doesn't matter if the garden is a place like your home or office, or a state of mind. Everything that we have discussed applies to both your physical and mental environment. Tend your garden and nurture successful crops. Pay careful attention to the seeds that you are sowing. Don't plant one thing and expect another to come up. Don't neglect your garden and let weeds of default grow. Choose your purpose and set your direction. Plant and nurture the seeds of your choices and take responsibility for creating your environment for success.

POINTS TO PONDER

* Everyone needs an environment or space where they can discover their possibilities. Do you have such a space? If not, can you create one?

* Do you pay more attention to your internal guides when you make choices, or are you listening to external influences?

* What can you change about *your* world that will have a positive impact on *the* world?

* Are you living in an environment full of compromises? If so, how can you remove them?

"SO LONG AS WE LOVE, WE SERVE. SO LONG
AS WE ARE LOVED BY OTHERS I WOULD SAY
WE ARE INDISPENSABLE; AND NO MAN
IS USELESS WHILE HE HAS A FRIEND."
ROBERT LOUIS STEVENSON

Chapter Seven
Who's In the Loop?
The People in Your Circle of Influence . . .
Who, Why, When and to What End?

Destiny Defined at Age 20

I was a senior in college, soon to graduate, and was considering several positions; however, I was not particularly passionate about any of them.

Then I heard about a one-day sales rally featuring four speakers. Since I was a sales major, I eagerly bought a ticket. I thought the rally would help me supplement my academic knowledge of sales. Little did I realize that my life would never be the same.

One of the speakers was Dr. Kenneth McFarland, "Dr. Mac," as I learned later many fondly called him. He was known as the Dean of American Speakers and was one of the most eloquent orators of the twentieth century. He also became a mentor after whom I patterned many of my values and key aspects of my career.

Dr. McFarland's speech was incredible. His style and eloquence mesmerized me. I literally felt chills down my back, and powerful positive emotions that let me know I had truly discovered my career path. Even before I jumped up to join the resounding standing ovation at the end of his speech, I was "hooked." I was not certain how or exactly where I would immediately fit into that business; I just knew I was on board!

Afterwards, I went up to the event sponsor, Dick Gardner, and with forceful and unbridled enthusiasm I told him I was ready to go to work for him. Three months later, I was speaking before small groups, selling enrollments to his sales seminars. Two years later, I started my own company. Ten years later, I was President of the National Speakers Association. I am still enjoying a wonderful and fulfilling career in speaking and training due to a simple choice I made, and an incredible person I met over thirty years ago. It was, to say the least, a life-enriching encounter.

Enriching Encounters in Your Environment

In the last chapter, we discussed the importance of creating

an environment for success. The people in your environment make a significant difference in your life. You can probably think of example after example of how someone totally altered the course of your life. In this chapter, we will cover how you can maximize the potential to enrich your life through your encounters with others.

Although I used a positive example in the story above, we can also enrich our lives with negative encounters. The people in our life can be one of the greatest sources of pleasure, pain, frustration and fulfillment. And we have the power to choose which role they will play. It all depends on how we respond to them and process what we learn.

Response–Ability

Throughout your life you will encounter people who are delightful and uplifting. You will also encounter people who may seem despicable and depressing. Surprisingly enough, the same person can, at different times, do a credible job of playing both roles. You might think that you should surround yourself with the former, and avoid the latter. Not really. I am a strong believer in the principle of, "It's not what happens to you, it's how you respond to what happens to you." Learning to respond appropriately to others is a key issue in learning how to create the life that you desire. We can learn from both of these types of people, respond appropriately to both, maximize the positive effects of our interactions with others and minimize the negative effects of our interactions with others.

A Look in the Mirror

In the world in general, things are not always as they seem. In dealing with people, things are almost never as they seem.

Here's an unusual guideline for understanding most people. Observe their actions, not their words, and realize that they should often be doing the opposite of what they are doing. We call this the "mirror technique," to help clarify and understand issues. If you look at something in a mirror, the image that you see is actually reversed. It is hard to tell that you are not seeing the "real" image, but you are not. That's why they paint ƎƆИA⊥UᗺMA on the front of most ambulances. As the ambulance approaches, you see the word "AMBULANCE" in your rear view mirror. It may sound odd, but I have discovered that people's mirror image is normally the one you see walking around.

In the case of the ambulance, reversing the image puts you on alert and helps prepare you to deal with a potentially dangerous situation. Often we need this same warning to help us deal with the people we encounter. They do things that intrigue us, confuse us, irritate us, and make us look for complex answers to explain their behavior. Sometimes the answer

The Contented Achiever

can be found by simply using the mirror technique. Try reversing their actions, and it may make much more sense. For example, a bully is undoubtedly insecure. A quiet person may be holding back anger. A confident, outgoing movie star could be painfully shy. A tough buyer may actually be looking for a salesperson strong enough to be a "partner." A teenager shouts, "I hate you," and is crying out for love and acceptance. Look at the opposite of the external image, and you may find you understand people much better.

> **WHEN YOU ARE ATTACKING SOMEONE, IMAGINE LOOKING IN A MIRROR. YOU MAY FIND YOU'RE ATTACKING THE OTHER PERSON FOR SOMETHING YOU DON'T LIKE ABOUT YOURSELF.**

Life is even better if you improve your understanding of why you behave the way you do. The mirror technique applies to you, too. When you are attacking someone, imagine looking in a mirror. You may find you're attacking the other person for something you don't like about yourself.

Now imagine what would happen if you actually tried having the opposite reaction. When you are clinging to something, especially something like anger or resentment, look in the mirror and see yourself letting it go. When you say something that causes you to experience negative emotions, look in the mirror and think about what you could have said. Usually

The Contented Achiever

saying the opposite will be more appropriate and create the effect you desire.

Get in the habit of "looking at yourself in the mirror" and pausing before you respond to people. You may decide that you want to reverse your response.

Back to children and their natural instincts. We come into the world with a good understanding of how to approach life, and we gradually become "mature" and start doing the opposite. Children know how to honestly respond to their feelings. We teach them to hide these feelings and show the world a false image of what is really going on inside them.

When things inside of you don't feel quite right, or you are uncomfortable with an interaction with another person, pause and consider using the mirror technique. Let it help guide you to an appropriate response.

Mother Nature Always Gets It Right

It's always interesting to study examples of man and Mother Nature interacting. Man is fairly consistent about getting things wrong, and Mother Nature is consistent about getting things right. Fishing is a great example of how man and Mother Nature interact, and it can provide you with a good model to test your actions.

The Contented Achiever

Imagine that you walk up to a clear pool or stream of water, and you can actually see an abundance of fish swimming in the water. Let's say you decide to catch a fish, so you reach into the water and try to grab one. What is likely to happen? Unless you have the reflexes of one of those bears you see in the nature films, you're going to be a frustrated fisherman. The fish will take off in all directions and you will come up empty handed.

To get really good at catching fish, you need to understand fish. Instead of repelling the fish by trying to grab them, you must learn what attracts them. What kind of food or bait attracts the fish you are trying to catch? Where are they likely to hang out? What water depth do they like? What type of vegetation do they like to be around? What water temperature do they enjoy? When you understand these things about a fish, you are in a much better position to be successful at catching them.

I personally know little about fish. That's why people like me can sit all day and not catch a fish, while someone who knows what they're doing can go to the right spot, use the right bait and catch exactly what they want in a very short time. They understand fish.

How can you use this to get the life you want? It's usually easier to see things in others rather than in yourself, so start out trying to identify "grabbers" around you. What are they doing to scare their "fish" away? How do they push positive things out of their lives?

Now for a surprise: The weaknesses you observe in others are often your greatest weaknesses. What are you trying to grab? How could you attract it instead? What do you need to learn to help you "make the catch?" Are you grabbing at money, a promotion, a relationship or anything else? You see these traits in others because they are consciously or subconsciously high on your mind. Compare the "fishing model" to your plan and see if you are attracting or grabbing.

I even talked with a counselor once who told me, "Any criticism you make of another person is a result of one of your own weaknesses." I didn't like him as much after he told me that, but he was probably right.

Sell-Fishing

One practical example of how to use the "Mother Nature Model" is for those of you who are involved in selling. That would be all of you by the way. You may not make a living selling but all of you have to sell something most every day of your life. Every time you open your mouth you want to be credible. Think of what you'd like to "catch" in life and who can help you learn to catch it. Are you trying to grab success or are you setting up the right conditions to attract it into your life? Take a closer look at those people who are grounded and seem to always operate at an even pace and still accomplish incredible things in life. They are experts at setting up conditions to attract success. They know how to fish.

Getting a Charge Out of Life

Although technology continues to heap time and energy saving devices upon us, I hear more and more people talking about being mentally and physically drained much of the time. For many, an abundance of stress is short-circuiting their success. What can we do to solve this problem?

Theoretically, each day is a new beginning. A chance to start over with your new day's supply of energy. Why do some people have more than enough energy to make it through the day and others start out the day with barely enough to get cranked up? Some people seem to be constantly recharged even though they are very active and others seemed to be drained even though they are inactive? Our levels of energy and stress are impacted strongly by the people around us.

Imagine that you have an energy source inside you that is similar to a car battery. When your battery is well charged, you can easily get started everyday and cruise through life. You have the power to maintain all of the critical systems and enough left over to run the stereo system and the other luxury items. But in order for all of the systems to work properly, you must constantly recharge the battery. You can operate on battery power for a while, but sooner or later, you need a recharge to keep all of the systems running properly. A properly running car has a source of power, usually an alternator or generator, which recharges the battery as you are actually using the car. But occasionally the electrical system will develop a "short" and slowly drain the battery power until the car can no longer be started. The people in your life can be alternators, generators or "shorts." They can help you generate the power that you need to function properly or they can be like electrical shorts and literally drain your energy. However, unlike the car, you have a choice. By choosing your response to others, you can choose whether or not another person will be an energy source or an energy drain for you. You may find that after you've been practicing for awhile, you will quickly spot energy drains like people who gossip, blame or constantly put out negative "vibes." They are not bad people, and you don't have to react or participate in their "game." What you may find, however, is that you choose to spend more and more time with energy boosters, and less time with energy drains.

> **BY CHOOSING YOUR RESPONSE TO OTHERS, YOU CAN CHOOSE WHETHER OR NOT ANOTHER PERSON WILL BE AN ENERGY SOURCE OR AN ENERGY DRAIN FOR YOU.**

The Contented Achiever

Bent Fenders and Angry Offenders

My friend Alan is, to put it mildly, a changed man. About a year ago, he chose to take a different path in life. Although Alan was highly successful in a financial sense, he felt as if he was running on battery power. His solution was to learn more about spirituality.

Characteristically, he approached his new interest with the same intensity that had made him highly successful in business. One of the first things he discovered was a new way to respond to people. He learned about empathy and compassion for others.

Here's what happened. One day it snowed and snowed and snowed. Alan was driving to work on icy roads, inching along, when someone in front of him slammed on the brakes. So did Alan. The person behind him did, too, but . . . Crunch!! Fenders were bent. Blood pressures soared and tempers flared. "Slow foot," the third link in the chain, bounded out of his car and launched an attack. The person who rear-ended Alan yelled, "What's wrong with you? Why'd you stop? Don't you know how to drive in the snow? (And worse!)"

One year ago, Alan would have countered with an offensive that would have made General Patton blush. His first instinct was to yell back and remind the guy who was at fault. But because he had learned some new options, that's not what he

The Contented Achiever

did. He looked at the other person with genuine concern and said, "Are you all right? Are you hurt?"

The other guy's anger fizzled. He calmed down. Both of the men then remained calm and had a reasonable discussion about how to handle the accident.

One year ago, Alan would have dumped more fuel on an already explosive situation. Instead, he decided to remain calm and respond more appropriately. Alan credits his transformation in part to the concept of not taking things personally. He had read this in *The Four Agreements*, an excellent book by don Miguel Ruiz, and tried it out for the first time with dramatic results.

Alan decided that he didn't need to develop anger and stress about issues that in the grand scheme of things didn't matter. His initial instincts and old habits almost made him join in the fray, but he practiced his new "role" and didn't take it personally. After all, the person in the rear car

IF YOU WANT TO TRULY CREATE THE LIFE THAT YOU DESIRE, YOU HAVE TO DESIGN YOUR PLAY OR DRAMA AND NOT GET CAUGHT UP IN THE DRAMA OF OTHERS.

didn't get up that morning and decide to have an accident with Alan. When he yelled at Alan, he was probably express-

ing his anger at himself for following too closely or not antici-
pating the slide.

The people you encounter often live life as if it were a play or
drama. They act the way they do because of their drama and
what is going on in their life. They are not out to get you. They
are simply responding the best they know how in the circumstances. If you want to truly create the life that you desire,
you have to design your play or drama and not get caught up
in the drama of others.

As for Alan, his personal drama now includes much higher
quality responses. Instead of letting the other person in this
situation drain his energy, he did the opposite. When he re-
layed this story to me he was thrilled with his new ability to
choose a positive response, and to actually be energized by
having the rear end of his car demolished! He was totally focused on the positive aspects of his experience. Admittedly,
this is one of those things that is easy to say and hard to do,
but the payoff in peace of mind is tremendous.

It's not what happens that is important, it's what you think,
say and do in response to what happens that's important.
Grounded, centered, enlightened people constantly learn how
to improve the quality of their responses to the events of life.
In doing this, they create a better life for themselves and those
in their circle of influence.

The Matrix of Life

Although Alan's accident may seem minor, you never know when such an incident may be significant. You may have played the game called *Six Degrees of Kevin Bacon*. The game consists of trying to connect any actor or actress to Kevin Bacon by creating a chain of relationships. There's seldom a situation where it takes more than six connections to get back to Kevin. For example, the actor chosen may not have been in a movie with Kevin; however, he was in a movie with another actor who in turn was in a movie with Kevin. A connection is made. Your life works in the same manner.

Years ago I learned a technique called mind-mapping that can improve your ability to think in a creative and organized manner. I read about it in a book titled *Using Both Sides of Your Brain* by Tony Buzan. It is a simple but amazingly powerful technique that will allow you to accomplish much more higher quality work in a fraction of the time it would take using more traditional methods. My life changed for the better the day I learned the technique. People in my loop asked about it, so I would show someone the basics and in many cases that was the end of that. They never got around to implementing it in their lives, but others saw it, learned it, implemented it and experienced very positive changes in their lives. Like the *Six Degrees of Kevin Bacon*, we established a connection from Tony Buzan through me to others.

The Contented Achiever

One particular friend in Memphis liked it so much he showed it to his wife, who was a schoolteacher. She shared it with her students. Once again, a strand of knowledge called mind-mapping connected us all. My friend and his wife were subsequently transferred to New York City, and she got a job teaching children of U. N. delegates. She shared mind-mapping with her students and was telling me how excited the children were about the technique and how quickly they learned it and began using it in their school assignments.

I can't help but think that some of these excited children went home to their parents and explained mind mapping to them. Thus, there is a possibility that mind-mapping could have spread internationally because of a chain of events that passed through my life. This simple chain of events that started with an idea that I read in a book could be a strand in the fabric that connects many people throughout the world.

The community of mankind is like a tapestry or matrix, and you are connected to people in more ways than you can imagine. You are probably no more than six degrees away from a lot more people than you think. (Including Kevin Bacon!)

You see, if you want to change the world, you can change the world. As a matter of fact, you have already changed the world, you just may not realize it. Your actions touch people, who touch people, who touch other people, and soon, the choices you have made reach all the way around the planet. Whether

The Contented Achiever

you know it or not. What kind of choices are you making? How are you affecting the world?

If you want to change the world, change yourself. Spread positive changes through the people in your loop, and then through the matrix that has the potential to connect everyone on the planet. Consider the following as you allow the lessons of life to flow through your matrix to others.

- Pay close attention to the people who are coming into your life. You can learn from all of them. Develop the attitude that everyone comes into your life for a reason. You may have to use the mirror technique to learn from some of them but you can learn from all of them. As a young person, I often learned the most from people who seemed to be poor managers, leaders or mentors. I learned what it was like to be on the other side of faulty thinking, words and actions. It helped me make the adjustments that I needed to make so I wouldn't pass on their habits to others as I became the manager, leader and mentor.

- Build relationships that are primarily based on what you want to learn from the other person, not on what you want to teach them. Teach by example and help when people ask for help. When someone is not ready to learn, it is not time to teach him or her. There is a wonderful passage from the Koran . . . "When the student is ready, the teacher will appear." Have a keen eye for your teachers, and be one yourself when you deem it appropriate.

The Contented Achiever

- Every so often you will encounter a person who has achieved mastery status related to a certain topic or talent. Be on the lookout for them and learn from them. Be aware that true masters often will not teach you unless you ask, so ask. First ask open-ended questions like, "What do I need to know?" and then listen.

- Don't expect masters to be masters at everything. Don't "throw the baby out with the bath water" because there's one aspect of their personality or life that you do not like. Einstein was admittedly a terrible family man. But he was a master at physics and many other topics.

- Gaining knowledge is just the first step to gaining wisdom. To convert knowledge to wisdom you must apply what you have learned. Learning to apply knowledge will put you on a path to mastery of a topic. You learn and teach best when you are applying knowledge.

Voicing Your Choices

It is astounding how much you can learn from others when you make learning a priority in your life. One of the best ways to improve your ability to learn from others is to let them know what you are trying to accomplish in life. Remember, no one can read your mind, especially since we are taught from a very young age to cover up our mistakes and act as if we already "know it all."

> **YOU'LL BE SURPRISED AT HOW MUCH MORE PEOPLE CAN AND ARE WILLING TO HELP YOU IF YOU LET THEM KNOW WHAT YOU ARE TRYING TO ACCOMPLISH.**

Others usually don't have any idea what you want or need in life. (Many times we don't even know!) The people in your circle of influence are often your best source of support, so it makes sense to let them know what you are trying to accomplish. Have you told your spouse or boss or others in a position to support you what success means to you? You'll be surprised at how much more people can and are willing to help you if you let them know what you are trying to accomplish. Be willing to earn their support but don't assume they are mind readers.

Since people rarely say what they truly mean, or feel, it is often difficult for others to know how they can help you. Make a list of your life choices and share the list with those in your inner circle of influence. Word of your choices will travel through the matrix of people that you know and don't know, and "coincidences" will quickly begin to occur that will support your choices. The events which will begin to unfold will seem remarkable. Position yourself appropriately for good times to happen to and for you.

When you share your choices and dreams with others, don't

The Contented Achiever

be disappointed when some people "rain on your parade." Fear, jealousy, discomfort with change, and other negative emotions often cause people to express resistance and even resentment. Let them choose their "drama" in life, but don't get caught up in it. Try to insulate yourself from those who are obsessed with guilt, blame and manipulation. People who are well grounded and centered don't let other people's negativity influence them. When you see negativity emerge, objectively observe it and learn from it. And let it go.

So Who Are You Going to Hang Out With?

Consider your circle of friends. How have they come into your life? Did they sort of show up, or are they there by design? We can indeed choose to a great degree who we want to spend our time with and have a meaningful friendship with. Those are important choices because, over time, they shape our lives, circumstances, opportunities and outcomes.

There is a lot to be said for being with people who cause us to grow, learn and progress. It goes without saying that we should choose friends and associates who personify high integrity and character and have worthy ideals.

Do you remember how your parents tried to impress upon you the importance of not running with the wrong crowd. That effort was probably even more important than they thought at the time. It has been said that in the teenage years, a person is constantly undergoing a process of becoming the average of the five closest friends he or she runs around with. If that is even close to true, these decisions are critically important throughout a lifetime.

Consider carefully the nature and specific details surrounding your life's goals. Are you frequently associating with people who are unlikely to have a positive impact on your goals and intentions? Give careful thought to who can have a positive impact on the meaning and advancement of your life's work. What appear to be minor decisions today can have enormous impact down the road.

A "Tremendous" Formula for Success

How many people do you know with the nickname "Tremendous"? I only know one: Charles E. "Tremendous" Jones. He is truly tremendous. Charlie gives the following piece of tremendous advice:

> **"YOU ARE THE SAME TODAY AS YOU'LL BE IN FIVE YEARS EXCEPT FOR TWO THINGS, THE PEOPLE YOU MEET AND THE BOOKS YOU READ."**
> CHARLES E. "TREMENDOUS" JONES

What better way to wrap up this chapter? If you want to play better golf or tennis, play with better opponents. If you want

to be a better musician, practice with someone who will stretch your current capabilities. If you want to be better at anything, associate with people who are better than you at whatever you choose to learn. Don't be the same in five years or in five weeks as you are today. Be conscious of who you have allowed to be in your loop!

Years ago, the people at Apple Computer talked about the value of pushing your limits. They stated that if you never got out on the edge and pushed your current limits, all you could hope for was "better sameness." A successful life is about ongoing improvement and personal growth. We are internally wired to learn and to pursue personal growth. You may not think you are; however, when you no longer pursue personal growth, the best you can hope for is "better sameness." There is no better way to push your limits than by taking positive advantage of the people in your loop.

> **THERE IS NO BETTER WAY TO PUSH YOUR LIMITS THAN BY TAKING POSITIVE ADVANTAGE OF THE PEOPLE IN YOUR LOOP.**

Give What You Get

Make a contribution to your "matrix." Be aware of who is in your loop and how far your personal matrix extends. Learn to

The Contented Achiever

respond appropriately to others. Draw energy from them and don't be drawn into their dramas. Experience the joy of mastery. Seek masters and become a master to others. Never lose sight of the fact that the next person that you meet may change your destiny . . . or you may change theirs.

POINTS TO PONDER

- Who have you encountered that totally altered the course of your life? Why?

- Who are your mentors?

- Whose mentor are you?

- What would people learn by observing your actions rather than your words?

- Like the person who tries to grab fish, what are you forcing in your life?

- Do you respond appropriately to negative circumstances in your life?

- Do you spend enough time deciding who you are going to invite into your inner circle?

- What are you doing today that could positively impact the matrix of your life?

"GO CONFIDENTLY IN THE DIRECTION OF YOUR
DREAMS! LIVE THE LIFE YOU HAVE IMAGINED.
AS YOU SIMPLIFY YOUR LIFE, THE LAWS OF
THE UNIVERSE WILL BE SIMPLER."
HENRY DAVID THOREAU

The Contented Achiever

Chapter Eight
Working the Puzzle of Life

Making Choices and Enjoying the Results

Imagine that you could go to a store and buy a puzzle called "This Is Your Life." The store offers several different kinds of puzzles: easy puzzles, difficult puzzles, two-sided puzzles, 3D puzzles and others. However, this puzzle, a puzzle about your life, is most unique. It allows you total freedom of choice about how you put it together. Every piece can be made to fit every other piece; it may not be the best fit, but you could find a way to make every piece fit every other piece.

The Metamorphic Cover

Our store even has one-year, five-year, twenty-year versions of your puzzle. As a matter of fact, you can pick one for any time frame you desire including one day, one hour or one minute.

The cover of the puzzle box changes depending on the time frame that you select, and it illustrates elements of your career, your hobbies, your relationships, and other important circumstances at that time. For example, if you bought the five-year version of the puzzle, the cover would show the circumstances of your life five years into the future and would change as you put each new piece in place.

Dump out the pieces and start to assemble them, and as you put the pieces in place you can see how each piece influences your future, with unlimited potential to change and reflect an infinite number of outcomes.

The Redo and Who-do Rules

There are only two rules for putting this puzzle together:

Rule #1: You can never redo a piece. Once you put a piece in place, you cannot change your mind. Even if you look at the future and don't like the results, you can't change that piece. The only way you can change the future outcome is with the next piece you select. The next piece has the potential to overcome the negative circumstances created by the last piece. This

The Contented Achiever

rule underlines the premise that all of life's decisions have consequences.

Rule #2: No one else can put a piece in place for you. Others
can give you suggestions, encourage or discourage
your choice, support your choice, make fun of your
choice or even warn or threaten you about certain
choices; however, in the end, you must take the action and put the piece in place.

By seeing your decisions and their results displayed immediately by this magic puzzle, you quickly begin to learn that
actions that you take in the present -- and only those actions
-- affect the outcome of your future. The puzzle may have a
hundred, five hundred or a thousand pieces; however, the only
piece you ever need to be concerned with is the one you are
dealing with right now -- the next piece.

As you work your "This Is Your Life" puzzle, you also quickly
discover that it is important to learn from the past and that it
is interesting to see the future. The only thing that really makes
any difference, though, the only thing that has any impact on
the future is what you are doing in the present. Over time, you
may get better and better at putting the next piece in place,
because your awareness has been heightened as to how present
choices influence your future.

The bad news is, you can't buy such a puzzle. The good news

The Contented Achiever

is that you already have such a puzzle and you don't have to buy it. It's the puzzle that we call your life and the pieces we call your life choices.

"From There to Here"

We talked in chapter three about being in a hurry to get from "here to there." Now that we've discovered how "here" affects "there," consider it for another moment.

If you are waiting to be happy until you are a little richer or thinner, or get your next promotion, or job, or car, home, wife, husband or whatever, you're in for a long wait. To enjoy peace of mind, as well as the greater probability of a fulfilled life, vow to live in the present. The following story says it well:

> *"First I was dying to finish high school and start college.*
> *And then I was dying to finish college and start working.*
> *And then I was dying to marry and have children.*
> *And then I was dying for my children to grow old enough*
> *for school so I could return to work.*
> *And then I was dying to retire.*
> *And now, I am dying . . . and suddenly I realize I forgot*
> *to live."*
>
> *-Anonymous*

The person in this poem spent so much time focusing on the "there" that they never experienced the joy of living in the

The Contented Achiever

"here." This is an unnecessary and unwise sacrifice.

Living for the future is just one form of being "there" centered. The other "there" is the past. People who live in the
past don't work the puzzle of life; they play the game of "if
only." "If only I'd taken that job . . . " "If only I'd had a
chance to go to this school . . . " "If only my family had lived
there . . . " If only I had or hadn't done this or that in the past,
I would be happy now. They rewind old tapes, replay old
scenes, regret old actions and remember old negatives and
live a life of relapses. Spend your energy replaying "if only"
tapes and you will soon drain your battery. Don't do it.

Here and now is the place to be if you want to create the life
you desire.

Informed Choices

Think of your life as a wonderful process of working on your
personal life puzzle on an ongoing basis. As the picture becomes clear, you are constantly being given the chance to
create the life you desire. Each new piece may represent a
new person coming into your life, a new opportunity, or a new
experience. Every circumstance bears on every other circumstance, and every choice has repercussions. It's like a giant
flow chart of life, with multiple "if this, then that" outcomes.
You will never have all the information on any subject. And

> TO BE HAPPY IN THIS LIFE, YOU TRULY MUST MAKE THE BEST CHOICES YOU CAN AS LIFE UNFOLDS.

you can drive yourself crazy trying to collect it all, delaying a decision until you are certain you know all the pros and cons. Your challenge is to make the best decision that you can, with the information you have right now, and focus on enjoying putting each piece in the puzzle. To be happy in this life, you truly must make the best choices you can as life unfolds, rather than adopt an attitude to "let the chips fall where they may." God has given us a gift -- freedom of choice -- that largely enables us to write our own scripts.

Sometimes the chips may not fall where you'd like. But even if you think you've done a poor job of putting the last piece in the puzzle, it doesn't really matter anymore. Your best next step is to concentrate on the pieces that are available at this moment. Enjoy the unfolding of your life. Each new piece can change your future. Each new day you have a new beginning and new choices.

It sounds so simple. If you want to move forward in life:

- Spend most of your time in the present.

- Consider your options.

The Contented Achiever

- Make an informed decision (a choice).

- Act on your decision.

- Learn from the consequences of your decisions.

But if it's so simple, then why do so many people struggle so much with this process? Many people complain about the poor hand they've been dealt and at the same time refuse to do anything about it. They spend so much time in the past and future that they do little to make good choices in the present.

Here, There, Everywhere

Wouldn't it be great if you could be in two places at once? Sorry. You can't. You probably understand that perfectly well in the physical sense, but do you also understand that the rule applies to your mental "location"? If you try to think of two different things at once, it will fracture your thinking process and destroy your focus.

- If you get mentally trapped or paralyzed by past circumstances and experiences, you can lose your ability to rationally consider your current options. That's because you simply cannot physically or mentally be in two places at once. If you are mentally in the past, you can't be in the present to choose your next puzzle piece. You must get from there (the past) to here (the present) if you want to create your future.

The Contented Achiever

- If you spend too much time living in the future, you will probably ignore the steps you need to take in the present to make the future come true. The future will not magically manifest itself unless you've surrounded yourself with the financial and human resources to make your dreams a reality. You must harmonize your future visions with current choices and actions. You're not finished when you "dream up" an exciting future. Living in the future can be a trap if you expect someone else to carry out the details of your vision.

It is not unusual, especially in a big organization, to hear people speak of what "the company" is going to do. I've got a secret for you; "the company" will never do anything. The people in a company do things. You cannot do a goal or a vision. You can only do an action that will result in the accomplishment of a goal or vision. If whatever someone tells you "the company" is going to do is truly important to you, ask them about the short-term focus of the project. Ask them who is doing what right now. Then ask yourself and other key players what you can do to help get the job done.

The Confession

It's time for a combination confession and public speaking lesson. Often when I give a speech, I make a planned humorous "error" early in the speech to put the audience at ease. Since so many people fear public speaking, they often have trouble identifying with people who are very comfortable speaking from the platform. The problem then, is that for a speaker to be effective, it is critical that the audience identify with them. I believe that a speaker who appears to be too slick will turn off a lot of their audience members. So sometimes I plan a harmless mistake. I don't try to hide it or act like it didn't happen. As a matter of fact, I do the opposite. I admit it, point it out and make fun of it. I want to appear to be very comfortable with the fact that I simply screwed up and it is no big deal. I want the audience members to think . . . hey, he's just like me! He's not perfect. It doesn't seem to bother him to just be honest about his mistake. I can identify with this speaker. I think I like this very human person.

I learned this trick from one of the world's greatest guitarists. He would mess up a guitar chord early in his performance. It would sound awful. He would stop the concert, turn to the audience and say:

> *"The music critics in the audience always come to my concerts and try to catch me making a mistake. I have learned to go ahead and make one early in the concert. That way they will have something to write about for their newspaper column. I get this out of the way and then they can settle back and enjoy the rest of the concert."*

It took me five or six concerts to realize that dumb-like-a-fox Chet Atkins was planning these screw-ups.

The authors of this book are just like you. We do not have any magic that keeps us from making mistakes. We fall into the traps that we write about. It is human to make mistakes. In fact, there is a good chance we'll learn as much or more than you from this book! Every day is an exercise of simply trying to take more steps forward than backwards. Learn to learn from your mistakes and even try to figure out ways to use them to your advantage. Above all, learn to recognize your mistakes, admit them, and correct them. When you find yourself in a hole, quit digging. If not, you will only find yourself standing in a deeper hole. Take corrective action and thoughtfully put the next piece of the puzzle in place.

The "We're Going to Write a Book" Trap

The three of us "talked" about writing this book for a long time. We would get so excited when we got together, energy would bounce off the walls. Talk, talk, talk, bounce, bounce, bounce. We bounced enough ideas around to write ten books, but no books magically appeared. When talk is all you do, excitement inevitably turns into frustration. We used all the standard excuses, and I won't go into them because you probably know them as well as we do. As a fellow human being, you know the feeling of not "walking your talk." We have all been there. You know what it is like to think that somehow you were going to "arrive without having made the trip!" We were in denial and the book was not happening.

One day, we decided to take our own advice. We realized that a book is made up of chapters that are made up of paragraphs that are made up of sentences that are made up of words. And words will not magically appear on the page of a

WHEN TALK IS ALL YOU DO, EXCITEMENT INEVITABLY TURNS INTO FRUSTRATION.

book unless someone takes action and writes them down. We clarified the steps necessary to produce this book, divided up the work, set deadlines, quit talking about it and started doing it. We launched the project, gained momentum, cruised through seven chapters and now we are bringing this project in for a landing. I am too embarrassed to tell you how much less time it has taken for us to actually write this book than we spent talking about it. We fell right into the trap. If we were cobblers, we would have had holes in our shoes. By the way, this was not a planned mistake. For a while I think we actually thought this book would happen if we talked about it enough. Can you identify with us? We hope you learn something from our lack of insight. Don't just talk about it, do it!

Go Ahead, Make My Choice!

I've talked to people who think that they have no control over

The Contented Achiever

their choices, and they believe that other people -- fathers, wives, bosses, friends -- can make choices for them. Somehow I'll bet Clint Eastwood never stared into the eyes of his protagonist and said, "Go ahead, make my choice." Earlier we talked about letting others make choices for you, such as what school you would attend, or what career you would pursue. In truth, we all make our own choices, even when we do it by default. Not making a choice is a choice. Letting others coerce you into decisions is a choice. Even a choice by default is a choice made by you.

Even if others could make a choice for you, why would you let them? This book is all about creating the life that you desire. Letting someone else make your choices would create the life that they desire for you. Some people think that by going along with the choices that others prefer will please others, and pleasing others is the right thing to do.

- "Going along" is a choice that was made by you.

- You can't please others if you don't please yourself. You cannot give away something you do not have.

- "You can't please all of the people all the time" and "You can't please many people much of the time." Stop making choices that are designed to please others if they do not please you. It is unhealthy and will not work in the long run. Our founding fathers got this concept right when they said in the Declaration of Independence that we are all entitled to "life, liberty and the pursuit of happiness."

Years ago, Viktor Frankl wrote a book called *Man's Search for Meaning* about his experiences in a Nazi death camp. The following passage is from the preface of this book:

> *In the concentration camp every circumstance conspires to make the prisoner lose his hold. All the familiar goals in life are snatched away. What alone remains is "the last of the human freedoms"—the ability to "choose one's attitude in a given set of circumstances."*

It would be difficult to read Dr. Frankl's book and not understand the power of choice in a person's life. Even in the worst circumstances, when it appeared that they had virtually no choices left, some of the prisoners realized that they could indeed choose their attitude. This decision would ultimately help many of them survive.

The World According to You

If no one can make choices for you, then logic dictates that you cannot make choices for others. Don't spend your time and energy trying to make choices for others. You can't do it with any long-term success. Stop trying. You can sell others on your choice or attempt to force them to pick your choice, but in the end, they must make their own choices.

Some of the most frustrated people on the planet are those who have misguidedly spent their time trying to control others. How many times have you had a salesperson try to sell you what they have instead of what you need? The really professional salespeople help you make good choices; they do not try to make choices for you. You can temporarily create the illusion that you are controlling someone else in a personal or work relationship but it will never last without someone paying a high price. Trying to take freedom of choice away from someone is never a good strategy. It is counterproductive to joy, productivity, creativity and fulfillment for everyone involved. Try to take people's freedom of choice away and most will eventually feel backed into a corner. Then their options are usually limited to fight or flight.

> YOU CAN TEMPORARILY CREATE THE ILLUSION THAT YOU ARE CONTROLLING SOMEONE ELSE IN A PERSONAL OR WORK RELATIONSHIP BUT IT WILL NEVER LAST WITHOUT SOMEONE PAYING A HIGH PRICE.

Failing to accept diversity of choice has caused many of the world's problems and may lead to the breakdown of a business relationship, a marriage or even ultimately result in something as catastrophic as a war between nations. Accepting diversity of choice leads to harmony.

The Contented Achiever

From a practical point of view, we are all very fortunate that people are not all alike. I am personally thankful that other people choose to be doctors, plumbers, electricians, sanitation workers, ozone-fixers, rocket scientists and all of the things that I do not want to be. The world would be a big mess if everyone wanted to be a leader and no one wanted to be a follower, or vice versa. Not only can we not make choices for others, I think we are better off because of it.

Suggestion: Devote the time you might have previously allocated to influencing other people's decisions to enhancing the quality of your own.

Enjoy the View While It Lasts

Most choices don't hang around forever waiting for you to decide what to do. People pass up opportunities to make critical choices and end up in circumstances that limit their options or make it appear as if they have no choices. For example, if you are a skydiver and forget to wear a parachute and subsequently jump out of an airplane, you have severely limited your present options. You passed up a very important choice when you were preparing for the jump. Your present options include panicking and spending the last few seconds of your life in terror, or enjoying the wind in your hair and the view while it lasts. Not a great situation to be in.

You may be able to let some little choices slip by and get away with it, but be aware of the "parachute" choices in life and don't let them slip by. Almost all crises are the result of passing up several choices that would have prevented them. Once again, Dr. Frankl's book reminds us of the millions of people who, through a multitude of tiny, seemingly insignificant choices, created a situation of unthinkable horror. What might have happened if even one person had made a different choice? How many chances were passed up over many years that could have changed the outcome of the "puzzle" we called World War II?

Can't I Just Rely on Good Luck?

To go through life relying on good luck is not a sufficiently sound success plan. You will probably have some of it, but you won't know when or about what, so don't count on it. You're better off becoming an insightful, proactive decision-maker who attempts to create much of his or her own destiny.

In a lifetime it is safe to say that we all experience some luck -- it comes to us in four types.

Type	Example
1. Good luck with meaningful consequences.	You or a loved one inherit a million dollars.
2. Good luck with lesser consequences.	The thunderstorm passes north of the golf course during your tournament.
3. Bad luck with lesser consequences.	The thunderstorm halts your golf tournament and it must be re-scheduled.
4. Bad luck with serious consequences.	You or a loved one are involved in a bad accident.

I wish you good luck with meaningful consequences, but in reality your life will probably deal you some of all four types at random times. I suggest that you give it your best shot every day in every endeavor and, over time, it will seem that you are manufacturing your own good luck. In truth, you will have proactively created positive results through good intent, appropriate skills and hard work. There is some truth to the old adage that . . .

"THE HARDER YOU WORK THE LUCKIER YOU GET!"

ANONYMOUS

The Contented Achiever

Certain people appear lucky, but in actuality they insightfully put themselves in the spot where luck is most likely to land. Many called Wayne Gretsky, the world-renowned hockey player, lucky. When asked why his timing always seemed so perfect, he said . . .

> **"I SKATE TO WHERE THE PUCK IS GOING TO BE --**
> **NOT TO WHERE IT HAS BEEN."**
> WAYNE GRETSKY

Long-Term Vision and Short-Term Focus

As I mentioned in chapter two, the best way to work a puzzle is to start by looking at the picture on the box. It is much better to start with a good overview of how the pieces fit in relation to each other. For example, let's say you are teaching your daughter to drive a car. In the first lesson she asks, "What's more important, knowing how to use the brake, the gas pedal or the clutch?" If you focus on primarily using the gas pedal you might find yourself always going "full speed ahead" and you would increase the chances that you will either wear out the engine quickly or crash. If you concentrate on using only the brake or the clutch, you'll never get started or gain momentum. All three are equally important and you must use them together if you want a smooth trip. Do you run your life using only the gas pedal? Do you specialize in using the brake or the clutch? Productive, centered people know how and when to use all three in harmony.

Harmonizing your focus and maintaining balance are keys to living a productive life. We talked earlier about visionaries who are excellent at looking into the future, and high-activity people who get a project going even though they are fuzzy on where it's headed. It's rare to find a person with a perfect balance between long-term vision and short-term focus, people who spend just the right amount of time in the past, present and future. Like the gas pedal, clutch and brake, knowledge of the past, present and future must be used in concert. Learn from the past, dream in the future and get things done in the present.

Puzzle Mastery

Throughout this book we have shared many ideas and concepts that we feel will help you create the life you desire. Most of them are highly effective and cost little or no money to implement. We believe all of these ideas have something in common: They will help you align your thoughts, words and actions with how you want to feel. Your feelings are your inner guides. Inner feelings are usually genuine and cannot be easily tricked. They ignore trying to please others, or trying to keep up with others' ideas about success. They are tuned in to your wants, desires and talents. They are constantly trying to help you make choices that support the best possible life for you. This is not a selfish posture we are recommending, but a process to help you on your path to becoming a Contented Achiever. You will be a far more positive influence on others you care about if you are successfully becoming the person you envision. Yes, your feelings should respect others, and yes, your choices should be appropriate. But they should also lead to freedom, growth and joy. Joy and feeling good may mean raising a child, painting, running a giant corporation, farming, writing, street cleaning or anything you decide. You must paint the picture on your puzzle box!

> **YOU WILL BE A FAR MORE POSITIVE INFLUENCE ON OTHERS YOU CARE ABOUT IF YOU ARE SUCCESSFULLY BECOMING THE PERSON YOU ENVISION.**

Some years ago I saw a mailman in New York City who had the job of picking up the mail out of a street-corner box. He gathered up the mail and took it to his truck. Then he took out a rag and walked back to the mailbox. Someone had spilled something on the mailbox and he cleaned it off. I looked around and saw all of the trash on the streets, and I couldn't believe that he took the time to clean off the mailbox. I was impressed. Over the past fifteen years, I have met many high-paid, high-powered executives. I have forgotten many of them, but I will never forget the Manhattan mailman. He taught me a lesson that has enriched my life for fifteen years. Whatever I was doing for a living, I wanted to be like him. I wanted to take pride in my work and seek joy in my life. I wanted my actions to speak louder than my words. I still don't know what made me stop and observe the mailman on that particular day, but I am glad I did. I have since learned to stop more often and watch the amazing events of the universe as they unfold.

"Aesthetic Arrest"

As I wind up this book, I want to share a wonderful story told by mythologist Joseph Campbell. It's about a space walk. An astronaut puts on his space suit and goes outside the main shuttlecraft. Suddenly he is struck by his circumstances. He is traveling through space at several thousand miles per hour in total silence. He looks in one direction and sees the moon. He looks in another direction and sees the Earth. He looks in other directions and sees the beauty of all the other celestial bodies. As he takes in the breathtaking circumstances unfolding before him he thinks, "What have I ever done to deserve this experience?" Campbell describes this as "aesthetic arrest."

It doesn't take a space walk to experience aesthetic arrest. It may be just a matter of watching your child play, looking at art, listening to music, reading a book, taking a walk in the woods, or watching an ordinary mailman do his job. Aesthetic arrest can happen anytime you're seeing the joy in the ordinary and extraordinary events of life as they unfold. Even though you may feel as if you are hurtling through space at thousands of miles per hour, you can create your own aesthetic arrest. Because the true aesthetic arrest in your world is your own life in all its glory. You create your life circumstances. There are many joys of life. And they are all yours to choose.

POINTS TO PONDER

- What is the most important piece that you need to put into place in the puzzle representing your life?
- If you put this piece in place, how will it affect your future?
- Are you trying to get from "here to there" or "there to here"?
- What have you been talking about for a long time that you really want to do?
- When are you going to do it?

Are You a Contented Achiever?

1. Do you have a clear idea of what you want in life right now?
   - ❏ Yes (5 pts.)
   - ❏ No (0)

2. How often do you take time alone to reflect?
   - ❏ Once a week (3)
   - ❏ Every so often (1)
   - ❏ Every day (5)
   - ❏ Never (-2)

3. Which of the following do you consider to be most important to your success?
   - ❏ Family satisfaction (3)
   - ❏ Financial achievement (3)
   - ❏ Personal fulfillment (4)
   - ❏ A comfortable home and other tangibles (3)
   - ❏ Helping others (3)
   - ❏ Freedom, growth and joy (5)

4. Do you have a plan to achieve what you want right now in life?
   - ❏ Yes (5)
   - ❏ No (0)

5. How would you describe your career?
   - ❏ Satisfying (3)
   - ❏ Boring (0)
   - ❏ Comfortably challenging (2)
   - ❏ Stressful (0)
   - ❏ Fun (4)

6. When an unusual opportunity presents itself, do you:
   - ❏ Evaluate how you feel about it and then decide whether to do it (4)
   - ❏ Analyze it carefully to determine all the pros and cons (2)
   - ❏ Dismiss it because it's unrealistic or you don't have time (0)
   - ❏ Go for it! (3)
   - ❏ Weigh the pros and cons, discuss it with friends, lie awake thinking about it, wait until you're forced to decide (0)

7. If your daily schedule has too many activities, do you:
   - ❏ Pause and evaluate each one to decide if it's worth investing your time in (4)
   - ❏ Try to do them all (0)
   - ❏ Get overwhelmed and panic (-5)
   - ❏ Pick the ones you enjoy the most and feel guilty about the rest (0)
   - ❏ Find a creative way to accomplish them all and still live the life you want (3)

The Contented Achiever

8. How do you react when something bad happens:
   - ❑ Determine your best response (4)
   - ❑ Fall apart (-2)
   - ❑ Try to figure out a way to resolve it (3)
   - ❑ Call trusted friends for input and then decide on a course of action (3)
   - ❑ Get professional advice (3)
   - ❑ Determine what the experience is trying to teach you (5)

9. Do you have a passion in life?
   - ❑ Yes (5)
   - ❑ No (0)

10. When was the last time you focused on your passion?
   - ❑ Last weekend (4)
   - ❑ Last month (3)
   - ❑ Today (5)
   - ❑ Last year (-5)
   - ❑ Don't have a passion, not applicable (0)

11. Where do you find answers to difficult issues?
   - ❑ Relying on inner guidance (5)
   - ❑ From books or other information sources (3)
   - ❑ Relying on parents' or others' experience (1)
   - ❑ With input from a few trusted advisors (4)
   - ❑ All of the above (4)

12. How would you describe the people you spend the most time with?
   - ❑ Draining (-5)
   - ❑ Energizing (5)
   - ❑ Supportive (5)

13. How would you describe the area where you spend most of your time (workspace or home)?
   - ❑ Neat (5)
   - ❑ Cluttered (-5)
   - ❑ Aesthetically pleasing (5)
   - ❑ Sterile (-5)

14. Do you have a place where you can be alone and reflect?
   - ❑ Yes (5)
   - ❑ No (0)

15. How do you respond to change?
   - ❑ Embrace it and look forward to learning from it (5)
   - ❑ Resist it and try to avoid it at all cost (-2)

16. Do you primarily live:
   - ❑ In the past (0)
   - ❑ In the present (5)
   - ❑ In the future (0)

17. Would others observe that your actions are in alignment with your words?
    ❑ Always (5)
    ❑ Most of the time (3)
    ❑ Never (-2)

18. Do you feel life is:
    ❑ A struggle in which you must fight for what you want (-5)
    ❑ A series of inevitable ups and downs (2)
    ❑ A manageable exercise (3)
    ❑ An exciting journey (5)

19. Is there something you've been talking about and wanting to do for a long time and haven't done?
    ❑ Yes (-5)
    ❑ No, I'm doing some of the things I want. (0)
    ❑ No, I'm doing all the things I want. (5)

Scoring

70-92

Congratulations! You're clearly headed for Contented Achiever status! The major struggles are behind you, and a few modifications can easily push you to the next level. Continue to spend more and more of your time on activities that create positive internal emotions.

50-70

You've seen what fun it can be to experiment with new beliefs and actually get results. Keep it up! No path is completely smooth, but yours is leveling out. You're almost ready to make the leap but in some areas you may be holding onto old patterns. A closer look may help clarify the obstacles you're encountering.

25-50

Congratulations on your awakening awareness. You recognize that there must be more to life and are clearly ready to take some steps. This is an exciting time of discovering new possibilities. Remember, you don't have to get there overnight, and every step will get you there even if indirectly.

25 and below

Yes, there is a better way, and believe it or not the journey can be exciting and fun! Your current discomfort will prove a great motivator. You may feel overwhelmed about the work ahead; don't overcomplicate things. Start with small steps.

CONSIDER THE FOLLOWING SUGGESTIONS TO CREATE A HAPPIER, MORE FULFILLING AND MORE PROFITABLE LIFE!

You've completed the assessment and determined your contentment status. Now it's time to take the next steps.

People are unique; therefore, paths to success must also be unique. Look at the questions where you scored low to see what's standing between you and complete freedom, growth and joy. Consider the following simple ideas, and choose the ones that are right for you in moving further along your path of being a Contented Achiever.

Properly Define Success

It is extremely easy to fall into the trap of letting other people define success for you. Bosses, co-workers, spouses, friends, parents, ministers, teachers, advertising executives and a plethora of other "counselors" are willing and eager to tell you what you should do with your life. Goals do not matter unless they matter to you. Define your own path in life!

From There to Here

This is another trap that can prevent you from being a Contented Achiever. Human nature has apparently hard-wired most of us to constantly strive to go from "here to there." It starts when we're children—-"Mom, Dad, are we almost there yet?" By definition, "there" is always somewhere or somewhen else. You can only be truly happy right now. Train yourself to mentally travel from the future to the present and have fun doing things in the present that will create an even better future.

Use Your Internal Guides

They go by many names: joy, happiness, contentment, anger, sorrow, anxiety or euphoria. They serve as excellent guides to tell you if you are on the right path or not. They are your emotions, your internal feelings, and they all fit into one of two basic categories . . . positive feelings and negative feelings. They tell you the truth when outside influences try to fool you. Pay attention to your feelings and let them help you find your best life path.

Plan Simply and Plan Effectively

Don't allow your plan to complicate your project or your life. Just make sure you include three critical steps. Be clear about the results you desire. Be honest about your current situation. Be diligent about developing and implementing specific action steps to propel you to success. Make a fluid commitment to your plan. Make the commitment to seriously carry out your plan, but remain willing to adjust your plan if circumstances change along the way.

Evaluate Your Beliefs

Your mind is chocked full of valid beliefs, invalid beliefs and everything in between. If you think that everything you believe is the "way it is" in the world, you are in for a surprise as you continue to learn and grow. Archie Bunker believed he was right all of the time. Others with low self-esteem believe they are wrong all of the time. Take inventory of your beliefs and determine which are serving you and which are holding you back. Let some beliefs go . . . and let some beliefs grow.

Clutter

Clutter is the root cause of many of your frustrations. Think of what your life would be like if you knew how to find things

The Contented Achiever

when you need them. If you decide it is easier to just "go buy another one" than find the one you know you have somewhere in your home or office, consider cleaning up and organizing the stuff in your life. What problems would go away for you if you didn't have to deal with your clutter or other people's clutter? Start big or start small, but start cleaning up today.

Become a "Space-Person"

Superman had his fortress of solitude. Batman had his bat cave. If these extraordinary people, with extraordinary powers, needed a place to reflect and get away from it all, why wouldn't you benefit from a special place called "your space"? It may be a room, a chair, a spot under a tree, an old washing machine box or any space. Stake a claim on your space today and become a genuine "space-person" for a few minutes each day. Create your own personal fortress of solitude.

People-Teachers

The people who come and go in your life often function like catalysts. When introduced into your environment, they may cause "reactions" that result in positive or negative changes for you. If you assume that everyone comes into your life for a reason, it becomes an interesting challenge to discover why each person is there, and what you should be learning from him or her. Pay attention to each of these valuable teachers.

The Next Best Step

Don't get ahead of yourself. Put your heart into your next project, and make a fluid commitment to a plan. But then take things one step at a time. Be prepared to adapt to change, because it will come. Stop between steps to make any necessary adjustments to compensate for changes in circumstances. Then get on with the next best step. By focusing on what's just ahead, you will avoid feeling overwhelmed and being too rigid in your thinking.

Time Passage Event Management

The 86,400 seconds you are given each day pass by regardless of what you are doing. You can't stop time, you can't save time, and you can't manage time. You can, however, manage events. Think of your day in terms of the events that you must focus on in order to call the day successful. Pause briefly between each event and think about your intent for the next event. That's all you really need to manage . . . the event and your intent.

The Snowball Effect

Negative feelings and thoughts are like snowflakes. They are easy to deal with when they first begin to fall, but if you ig-

The Contented Achiever

nore them they can become an avalanche. A healthy mental response can melt negative snowflakes before they become a mind-and-life altering avalanche. Remember, it's not what happens to you, it's how you respond to it that matters. Handle the snowflakes yourself or ask for help. This is one case where you do not want to "have a ball."

The Puzzle Called Life

Life is like putting together a jigsaw puzzle, except you can't "take a piece back." What's done is done. For example, you can't un-insult someone. Unlike a regular puzzle, the outcome of your life-puzzle changes with each piece you play. Forget the pieces you played in the past and focus on the pieces in your hand. They are the only ones that have the potential to make a difference in your life-puzzle.

About the Authors

Don Hutson

Don Hutson is founder, Chairman and CEO of U.S. Learning. He is author of *The Sale*, co-author of six other books, and has over 5,000 speaking appearances to his credit. He is internationally acclaimed in the fields of sales, leadership and employee motivation.

Chris Crouch

Chris Crouch is Executive Vice President of U.S. Learning. His career reflects impressive success in both finance and personal development initiatives. While he has developed and implemented cutting-edge training programs, his passion is writing.

George Lucas

George Lucas, Ph.D., is President and Chief Operating Officer of U.S. Learning. George's experience as an educator, consultant and seminar speaker gives his audiences and readers a valuable perspective on success. He specializes in marketing strategies and negotiations.

U.S. Learning is based in Memphis, Tennessee and its website address is www.USLearning.com.